Better Homes and Gardens®

FENCES & GATES

A DO-IT-YOURSELF GUIDE TO DESIGN AND CONSTRUCTION

Meredith® Books
Des Moines, Iowa

Better Homes and Gardens Fences and Gates
Editor: Ken Sidey
Writer: Martin Miller
Copy Chief: Terri Fredrickson
Publishing Operations Manager: Karen Schirm
Senior Editor, Asset and Information Manager: Phillip Morgan
Edit and Design Production Coordinator: Mary Lee Gavin
Editorial and Design Assistant: Renee E. McAtee
Book Production Managers: Pam Kvitne, Marjorie J. Schenkelberg,
    Rick von Holdt, Mark Weaver
Contributing Copy Editor: Don Gulbrandsen
Technical Reviewer: Griffin Wall
Contributing Proofreaders: Janet Anderson, David Craft, David Krause,
    Maureen Patterson
Indexer: Donald Glassman

Additional Editorial Contributions from
Abramowitz Design
Publishing Director/Designer: Tim Abramowitz
Designer: Joel Wires
Photo Researcher: Amber Jones
Photography: Image Studios
    Account Executive: Lisa Egan
    Project Coordinators: Deb Jack, Karla Kaphaem, Vicki Sumwalt
    Director of Photography: Bill Rein
    Photographers: Will Croff, Dave Classon, Scott Ehlers,
        Glen Hartjes, Shane Van Boxel, John von Dorn
    Assistants: Mike Clines, Mike Croatt, Max Hermans,
        Bill Kapinski, Roger Wilmers
    Technical Advisor: Rick Nadke
Additional Photography: Doug Hetherington
Illustration: Art Rep Services, Inc.
    Director: Chip Nadeau
    Illustrator: Dave Brandon

Meredith® Books
Executive Director, Editorial: Gregory H. Kayko
Executive Director, Design: Matt Strelecki
Executive Editor/Group Manager: Larry Erickson
Senior Associate Design Director: Tom Wegner
Marketing Product Manager: Isaac Petersen

Publisher and Editor in Chief: James D. Blume
Editorial Director: Linda Raglan Cunningham
Executive Director, New Business Development: Todd M. Davis
Executive Director, Sales: Ken Zagor
Director, Operations: George A. Susral
Director, Production: Douglas M. Johnston
Director, Marketing: Amy Nichols
Business Director: Jim Leonard

Vice President and General Manager: Douglas J. Guendel

Meredith Publishing Group
President: Jack Griffin
Executive Vice President: Bob Mate

Meredith Corporation
Chairman and Chief Executive Officer: William T. Kerr
President and Chief Operating Officer: Stephen M. Lacy

In Memoriam: E. T. Meredith III (1933-2003)

All of us at Meredith® Books are dedicated to
providing you with the information and ideas you
need to enhance your home and garden. We welcome
your comments and suggestions. Write to us at:
Meredith Books
Home Improvement Books Department
1716 Locust St.
Des Moines, IA 50309–3023

If you would like to purchase any of our home
improvement, gardening, cooking, crafts, or home
decorating and design books, check wherever quality
books are sold. Or visit us at: bhgbooks.com

Note to the Readers: Due to differing conditions,
tools, and individual skills, Meredith Corporation
assumes no responsibility for any damages, injuries
suffered, or losses incurred as a result of following the
information published in this book. Before beginning
any project, review the instructions carefully, and if
any doubts or questions remain, consult local experts
or authorities. Because codes and regulations vary
greatly, you always should check with authorities to
ensure that your project complies with all applicable
local codes and regulations. Always read and observe
all of the safety precautions provided by
manufacturers of any tools, equipment, or supplies,
and follow all accepted safety procedures.

TABLE OF CONTENTS

CHAPTER HIGHLIGHTS

Every fence has a job to do—
perhaps several at once. To build the
right fence in your yard, you must
first be sure what you want it to
accomplish. This chapter discusses
those functions and will provide you
with concrete suggestions on how
you can choose the fence that will
meet your needs.

FENCES AND FUNCTIONS

A new fence is more than just an additional structure in your landscape. It not only alters your yard, it can have a major impact on both you and your neighbors. A garden fence, for example, will forever change the way you travel through your landscape. Front yard pickets will somehow make your house look different, even though the fence is 50 feet away. And a privacy fence or a boundary-line marker can quickly become an issue because, like all issues, it has two sides. You may like the side you see; the neighbors may not like theirs.

For better or worse, once you've built them, fences make contributions you have to live with for a long time; that means their design, materials, and construction should reflect careful planning.

Good planning and perhaps a little advance public relations in the neighborhood will take care of these potential problems. What's most important is that you base all your fencing decisions on the answer to one question: What do I want the fence to do? This chapter presents you with the information you need to answer it.

BOUNDARY FENCES

▲ **Boundary fences can be marvels of multi-tasking. This handsome fence defines space, protects privacy, and enhances the style of the yard.**

The need to define ownership and the beginning and end of property isn't "as old as the hills"—but almost. And what better way is there to set off what's yours from what's not than a fence?

Boundary fences organize space, both at the edges of a property and within it. What they look like and how you build them depends on their location and the job you want them to do.

▶ **Post and rail fencing may not be a means of privacy or security, but it is an affordable way to designate boundaries, and it fits architecturally with the lay of the land.**

Front yard fences

Front yard fences typically have more than one function. While they must define the edges of a property, they often have to do so in a way that seems inviting. They have to make a design statement that says, "This is ours; come in." They usually don't have to provide much security or privacy, just a measure of containment—for children and pets. What's more, they have to do all that with a style that complements the house (and often, the neighborhood).

A front yard fence is usually 3 to 4 feet tall—shorter than a backyard fence. A front yard fence taller than that can look out of place in the neighborhood.

Where security, privacy, or containment is not high on your priority list, consider a rail

◀ Fencing can be used to provide subtle definition between spaces. This fence establishes a separation between the deck and garden, yet with its wide opening, also invites one into both spaces.

fence. Even hand-hewn rustic rails go well with most architectural designs. If you need containment and a little more security, picket and chain link fences are good choices. So are ornamental metal fences. They keep children and animals from running out of the yard and impart a sense of security.

Backyard fences

Backyard fences have a different purpose—or a different combination of purposes. They need to mark lot lines, but because most outdoor activities now take place in backyards, they also need to provide security and privacy. Those functions call for taller fences than front yard structures—6 feet is common—and generally closed surfaces. That's why you'll find any number of board-fence styles in backyards. Paling, stake, and siding fences also make

good choices and bring a nontraditional element into the landscape design. Combine any of these materials with lattice or louvered panels on top or in alternating bays and you'll open up the design without sacrificing much privacy.

WHERE'S THE PROPERTY LINE?

On most properties, locating the lot line can take a little detective work. Whatever marker was put there originally may be gone or hidden by an overgrowth of grasses.

In most cases you're looking for metal spikes or pipes. If you can't find them easily, a rented metal detector can often do the trick. Make sure you pinpoint all the markers; don't assume your property is square. When you do find them, replace each one with a 2-foot length of galvanized pipe. Drive it until it's slightly above grade—so it won't interfere with mowing the grass.

BOUNDARY FENCES (CONTINUED)

Backyard fences offer a little more freedom in planning their design because you won't need to be as concerned with neighborhood styles as in a front yard.

Defining spaces

▼ **Good neighbor fencing has the same look from both sides. This low iron fence and gate offers a consistent design from all angles and protects the front lawn and garden from any unwanted foot traffic.**

Lot lines aren't the only kind of boundary to define. Within the interior of your yard, you'll want to separate spaces from each other. For example, a patio that spills out into a wide expanse of yard may feel too open for intimate dining. A fence, even a low one, can help contain the space and establish the right mood for areas devoted to entertainment. Fences can keep utility areas from encroaching on

▲ Property line fencing helps create a private sanctuary within its borders. A fence like this could be overbearing for a neighbor or the aesthetics of the neighborhood—keep these factors in mind when designing your fence.

recreation zones. They can hide storage areas or waste containers. They help isolate relaxation retreats and separate entertainment areas from garden plots.

Many interior fences are low fences. A one-rail fence no higher than 18 inches may be all you need to define the edges of your planting beds.

Tall screens, which are often built with open infill (lattice, for example) can screen out garbage cans or put an unsightly storage shed out of sight. Open patterns will hide what's behind them without completely interrupting the rhythm of the overall landscape. Besides, they are a natural haven for climbing vines.

Scales and rhythms

Property line fences are usually the longest in a yard, and that means they can have a major visual impact on the landscape. The variety of materials, as well as their sizes and shapes, creates unique visual rhythms and proportions—all the more so over the expanse of a boundary fence.

For example, on a short run, large posts and rails look strong and sturdy. Spread down a long lot line, however, they can look massive and overbearing. But you can soften them and add visual interest with small details like decorative

▲ Tall property line fencing can appear daunting. The attention to detail in the gate of this fence helps to make it more appealing and friendly.

trim. Post spacing—though dictated primarily by structural requirements—helps define the rhythm of a fence design. Short spacing moves the viewer's eye rapidly down the fence line. Wide spacing (which may require larger framing) will slow down the rhythm.

▲ Architectural detail can be added to property line fencing to soften its appearance. This open arbor and flowering plants help provide a welcoming entrance and set the stage for what will be found inside.

MARKING UTILITIES

Although it's obvious that aboveground obstacles, such as trees and rocks, will affect the installation of your fence, so can things located underground. Water and gas lines and electrical and telephone cables may keep you from putting your fence just where you want. Before you start digging postholes—actually, before you finalize the location of the fence—call your utility companies. Most firms will flag the location of their lines at no cost. Leave the flags in until your planning is done.

SECURITY FENCES

Security comes in different forms, with different meanings. Applied to fencing, it can mean keeping things out or keeping them in–or both, because a fence can't really do one without the other. Both your construction methods and your material choices will hinge on what you want it to do.

Keeping things in

You have many choices of materials if your primary goal is keeping toddlers in the yard. You should look for fencing that's high enough (at least 4 feet) and open, so you can always keep an eye on them from any angle.

▲ To keep small children inside, fencing should be at least 4 feet in height. A solid board and batten fence like this one would be good for keeping in pets as well.

Picket fences are good for front yards; so are ornamental fences with closely spaced infill (but check building codes first–codes always regulate fence and rail spacings). Chain link will work anywhere, but not necessarily with older children–it makes great toeholds for climbing. Chain link and wire mesh are also effective for containing smaller pets; they can't gnaw or scratch it.

Keeping things out

Keeping intruders out of your property requires different methods and materials. This type of security fence needs to be tall, sturdy, and hard to climb. High, solid board fences are one

▲ Ornamental iron fencing can be both elegant and provide substantial security. The finials on this fence add height and make the fence more difficult to climb.

suitable style. They also possess a built-in psychological deterrent–they prove effective, in part, because intruders can't see what's on the other side.

Solid board fences also make a space feel completely private–and confining, so you may want to think twice about employing this design without modifying it. For example, you can make a security fence feel less like a stockade by incorporating small lattice windows in the infill or open panels on top of the fence, out of reach. Your design will be stylish and you won't feel like a prisoner in your backyard.

Solid security fences also come with an unintended consequence. Just as intruders can't see in, they can't be seen from the outside if they do get in. For this reason you should not expect a board fence (any fence, for that matter) to be the only thing that secures your property. lways install motion-sensing lighting and alarms in conjunctioAn with the fence.

For all of the above reasons, you may want to consider a wrought-iron or tubular-steel security fence with narrow infill spacing. Both of these materials allow adequate visibility from the outside and are strong enough to resist break-ins. Metal fences don't come with handholds or footholds and can be constructed tall enough (5 feet is a minimum; 6 feet or more is better) to discourage climbing without compromising their natural elegance.

EXPECT A SETBACK

Almost all municipalities enact building codes and zoning ordinances. Building codes are designed to ensure the safety of a structure by regulating the materials used and construction methods employed. Some communities will have specifications for fences, including posthole depths, footing requirements, and material choices.

Zoning ordinances regulate how a property is used, and among other things they establish maximum heights for structures (sometimes fences) and how far your fence needs to be inside your property line. This distance is called the "setback," and virtually every community requires one.

So if you've planned to put your fence right on the property line, or even 6 inches inside it, you may be in violation of a local regulation. Zoning officials have the power to make you remove an improperly located fence.

Check with your local building and zoning departments both before you start designing your fence and after you've drawn the plans.

◄ Wrought-iron fencing is offered in a variety of styles and can easily be customized to match the architectural detail of a home. This wrought-iron fence and security gate has narrow infill spacing and the height to discourage intruders.

Keeping out four-legged "friends"

If you live in or near a wooded area, you may be visited from time to time by one of nature's most graceful—and hungry—creatures. Don't be misled by the presence of deer. They're not looking for conversation. If they're in your yard, they're after a snack. Gorgeous as they are, they can wreak havoc on your garden or planting bed.

Deer don't like confined spaces, and they don't like noise. The most effective way to keep deer out is to build something high enough to dissuade them from jumping. In most cases, nothing less than 8 feet will do. Depending on the location of your garden, the overall style of your landscape, and your budget, a woven wire fence will keep them out, but it won't look stylish.

Smaller openings will also keep out smaller pests. Whatever wire you use, set the posts on 10-foot centers, staple the wire to the posts, and stake or bury the bottom.

Some small-plot gardeners have eliminated deer feeding by tying plastic grocery bags to rope or wire strung between posts. When even the slightest breeze blows, the bags make a rustling noise that deer seem to fear. No matter what you do, clear tall brush and weeds away from the perimeter of your garden fence.

If neighborhood dogs are the problem (or if

▶ The lattice work and trellis, in combination with the mature vines, add visual interest and privacy to an otherwise typical white picket fence. The flowering plants invite visitors into the garden.

you need to keep your own dog contained), build a fence that dogs can't get through, jump over, or burrow under. A 6-foot fence should keep a large breed inside (or out); a 4-foot fence is tall enough for smaller dogs. In both cases bury the fence (wire is a good choice) at least 6 inches deep to thwart tunnelers.

▶ Solid wood fencing of significant height can deter intruders because they can't see what's on the other side. Brick columns flank this gate and help to break up the monotony of the long fence line.

FENCING A POOL

Security becomes a specialized problem with swimming pools. If you have one and your yard can be accessed by children—both your own and the neighbors'—make sure its fence won't let them in when no one's watching. Build it so they can't climb over or under it, or slip through its infill.

A swimming pool fence should allow clear visibility from outside into the pool—chain link meets that criterion, but is easy to climb. Picket fences and clear acrylic panels are good choices. So are tall ornamental metal fences.

Be sure to check your local codes for requirements governing swimming pool fences. Most codes require self-closing and self-latching gates.

Don't forget your spa or garden pond—many communities define these as safety hazards that require a fenced enclosure.

FENCING FOR PRIVACY

Creating privacy means blocking views, and there are many fences ideally suited for this job.

Develop a privacy strategy

The most common error made when planning a privacy fence is making too much of it. Privacy is best planned strategically, a little bit at a time. For example, if your neighbors can see into your backyard from only one limited angle, then you only need a privacy structure that blocks the view from that angle. You don't need a whole fence line when a bay or two will do.

To create strategic privacy in a fence that runs the length of your lot line, build tall sections where you want total privacy and short sections where you want to preserve the view. The changing heights of the

design also make the fence more appealing. Or you can install lattice sections (or clear materials, such as acrylic) in the solid infill to let in views where privacy is not needed. Such variations allow the fence (and you) to breathe.

Before considering what kind of fence to build, take an inventory of your landscape. Stand or sit in the spaces you commonly use and look around you. Make notes on a sketch of your yard with arrows designating the points from which you're visible.

Before you get out your planning tools,

▶ Lattice screening can serve many purposes—it can be strategically placed to give privacy to a hot tub or hide unsightly garbage bins, or as shown here, teamed with a vine type plant, it can simply be a decorative element in the outdoor garden.

consider the placement of any privacy structure. You'll get more privacy from a structure that's close to an activity, and less from one that's far away.

Privacy and purpose

The one rule to follow when planning for privacy is this: All spaces do not need it equally. Each area of your landscape has different uses, and you should tailor an area's need for privacy to its use.

For example, a quiet spot for reading, contemplation, or intimate dining should feel secluded. So should your swimming pool and spa. Such spots need maximum privacy, the kind that comes from tall fences.

Because your needs will be different, however, entertainment space out on a deck or patio or the area where children play can be more open. Parties don't need to be as private, in part because the activity itself consumes everyone's attention. With all kinds of people attending, it's quasi "public" anyway. In general, such open spaces will be sufficiently secluded with latticework screens or fencing with an open infill pattern.

Good privacy fences

Solid fences will definitely block out views (as well as enhance security), but they have several built-in drawbacks.

▲ Fencing should work with the space it's protecting and the surrounding landscape. Solid wood fencing by this patio would take away from the landscape and overpower the space. This louvered fence adds style and still provides security and privacy.

In small spaces they can seem imposing, and over a long fence line they're just not very interesting. They also create strong downdrafts instead of blocking the wind and can cast shadows that may cause too much cooling in the areas they're designed to protect. You want a structure that gives you privacy with style and comfort.

Louvers and lattice make excellent privacy screens. Lattice may not block out views entirely, but the pattern of the lattice acts to distract the view, if not block it.

Louvers behave similarly, their vertical lines calling attention to themselves but not completely blocking the view. The angle of the louvers also restricts full views and offers only partial visibility.

A louvered fence can behave somewhat differently in a front yard than a backyard, however—not because of the location, but because of traffic. Passengers in a car passing a louvered fence just at the right speed will be able to see right through it.

▲ Fencing with open slats still allows some light to filter through, and if it's horizontal, it is completely private—providing a sense of openness that solid wood fencing cannot.

▲ Board-on-board fencing provides a great deal of privacy and is difficult to climb. You can alternate the installation of the boards for narrower slats.

◄ Picket fencing is easy to install and it can take on a personality of its own with architectural details and paint or stain. This white picket fence establishes boundaries and lends some privacy to this backyard garden.

Horizontal louvers, however, don't display this characteristic. In fact, horizontal louvers are view proof–the only things you can see on the other side of the fence, even if you're standing right next to it, are the sky and a few treetops.

Borrowing from the principle of lattice and louvers, any fence whose infill pattern contains open spaces in an eye-catching pattern can function as a privacy fence. Alternating boards and slats and leaving narrow spaces between them, letting the tops of the infill run wild and varying their spacing, and board-on-board fences are all designs that will deliver filtered privacy with substantial visual interest.

At a minimum, if you must have a solid board fence, you can enhance its appearance with trellises and climbing vines, random "window box" display shelves, and other accents.

CONTROLLING NOISE

On the surface, noise might not seem to be a privacy issue, but it is. Noise is essentially an aural invasion of your space. Even if you build a fence to enhance security or define a boundary, certain styles make better noise barriers than others.

As a general rule, the thicker and more dense the material, the more effective it is in muffling sound. That would exclude solid board or board-on-board fences as efficient noise-reduction fences. Board-and-batten and featherboard fences are more effective. Their surfaces have irregular planes that break up and scatter the sound waves.

Plywood and tongue-and-groove fences are slightly better, but high siding fences shingled or sided on two sides will do the best job. That's because the enclosure between the two sides absorbs some of the sound, and the surface deflects it.

CREATING COMFORT ZONES

You might not think of a fence as an agent of climate control, but the right fence in the right location can have a major effect when it comes to making an outdoor space comfortable.

Fences can help make shade, tame strong winds, and keep snow from drifting across your property and rendering it impassible. In short, fences can help create microclimates in your yard—small, localized areas in which the temperature, sun patterns, and wind velocities differ from the general conditions. To take advantage of this characteristic, you'll need to inventory your landscape.

▲ Louvered fencing adds visual interest and creates filtered shade. In addition to the open slats in this fence, the open top helps disperse the wind providing additional protection from the wind 6 to 12 feet from the fence.

WINDSCREEN HEIGHTS

Wind protection drops off at a distance approximately equal to the height of the fence.

Solid Fence

6'
6'
12'
0'

Solid Fence with Open Top

12'
6'
6'
0'

An open top diffuses the wind and provides wind protection 6' to 12' from the fence.

Taking inventory

If you want fencing to increase shade, plot the course of the sun across your yard. Stake out shade patterns at different times of the day. Include prevailing winds and seasonal breezes in a wind study. Streamers tied to stakes will help reveal changing wind currents in your yard.

To turn all this information into practical use, identify the areas you want to protect and note them on a sketch.

Making shade

How much shade a fence creates depends on its height, how close it is to the shaded area, and whether its orientation is parallel or perpendicular to the sun. The goal of making shade, however, is to create filtered shade, not to cast a surface into total darkness. This makes lattice panels and louvers—and all fences with open patterns—good candidates when you need shade on a low area.

Fences will reflect light too. If you paint the sunlit side of your fence a light color, sunlight (and heat) will bounce into a nearby deck or patio and make it useable a little earlier in the year.

Filtering the wind

Unlike light, wind doesn't bounce off objects. It spills over them and drops back down into your deck or patio space—if the object is a solid fence (see illustration, opposite). Fences that divert or break up the wind provide better wind control. A louvered fence changes the direction of the wind and can eliminate the debris-filled eddies caused by wind trapped inside a corner.

The open surface of board-on-board fences, grape-stake fences, spaced-slat fences, and basket-weave and lattice fences filters the wind and lets it through in a pleasant breeze instead of causing it to vault over the fence and come down with a vengeance.

▲ Fencing installed on the south and west sides of a garden will give it afternoon shade. The same fencing at the edge of a deck or patio could cause the area to become overly cool. Move the fencing to the other side and paint it a light color and it will radiate heat.

▶ If you need to keep snow from drifting across your property, build a Wyoming snow fence. Made of 1x6s spaced 6 inches apart starting 10 inches above the ground, a Wyoming snow fence will last 25 years or more. It is as effective as plastic and requires minimal maintenance.

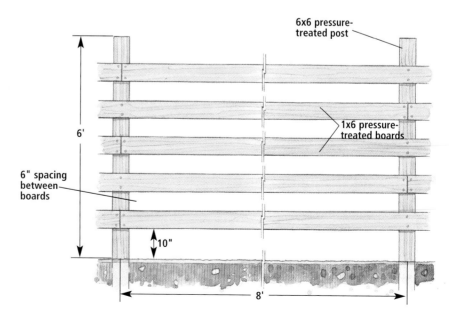

6x6 pressure-treated post

1x6 pressure-treated boards

6' · 6" spacing between boards · 10" · 8'

DRAWING PLANS

▶ You won't need a large collection of tools to make a good fencing plan, just a few drafting tools and graph paper with ¼-inch squares.

When you need to ensure that your final fence design will meet all your expectations, nothing beats pencil and paper (and perhaps a few drafting tools). Paper plans take all of the information you've been gathering and put it in one place. How elaborate you make the plans will depend on how complicated and extensive your fence(s) will be.

At a minimum, for a single fence you should have a sketch of your property that shows its major architectural features–the house, garage, storage sheds, and existing trees. This sketch should also include the property line, the location and distance of the new fence from the lot line and the house, and other pertinent details, such as post spacing.

For simple fence lines you probably don't need a scaled drawing. For landscape plans that will feature more than one fence or in which fences play a part in a landscape makeover, your rough sketch is the first step. In actuality, it will become the basis for a base map.

A *base map* is an overhead view of your property drawn on scaled graph paper that shows the features noted previously, as well as all pertinent measurements between them. This base map will resemble the plat map you received when you bought the property, and it will function as the basis for the rest of your plan.

A fully developed landscape plan will evolve from a set of tracing paper sheets, each of which

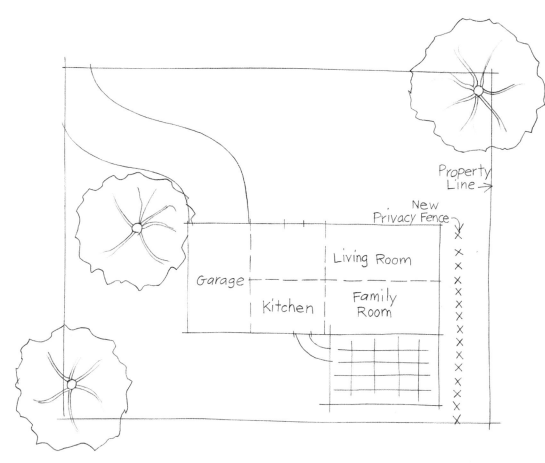

Property Line →

New Privacy Fence →

Living Room

Garage

Kitchen

Family Room

◄ At a minimum, a basic fence-line sketch should include the property line, structures such as the house and outbuildings, and existing trees. More elaborate designs should be drawn to scale.

has a different job to do. A *site analysis* might include sun and wind patterns, traffic flow, any changes or enhancements you want to make to activity areas, and comments about how fencing can help make those changes. You might draw *bubble plans,* which will give you a way of experimenting with how you want to use various areas in your yard.

Your *final fencing plan* will complete the process, with dimensions and notes about each of the structures and fences you intend to build. Finally, for each fence you should draw a *bay plan*—a rendering that illustrates the details of fence construction. Bay plans help when it comes to making materials lists and estimating costs; they also serve as working drawings—the instruction sheet—for building the fence.

No matter how sophisticated you make your plans, you should always start with actual measurements made in the field—your yard. Using your rough sketch and a 100-foot steel tape, measure the perimeter of your site, the size of its permanent features, and the distances between them. Record the dimensions on the sketch. Then take everything back inside and add your proposed fence lines. If you change any of the measurements that affect the fence, go back out and check to make sure there's nothing that will interfere with your new concepts. Don't worry if your drawing doesn't look like an architect drew it; if it's accurate and legible, it will work.

CHAPTER HIGHLIGHTS

Whether you want a fancy fence or a

functional one, this chapter will help

you build it. You'll find step-by-step

instructions for building many different

kinds of fences, as well as suggestions

for customizing your design.

BUILDING FENCES

Fences are not made just with lumber–a good fence will contain precise measurements, straight cuts, and immovable joints. All these characteristics will not only make your fence look like it was put together by a pro, but they also will make it last longer.

All fences go up in the same order, and that establishes a certain routine to the work. Routine is good–it lets you concentrate on the more important aspects of building the fence, the things that require decisions. But there are other things you can do to minimize distractions and stay focused, and they're remarkably simple.

First, if you haven't done so already make a list of all the steps involved in building the fence. Include the obvious tasks, such as "Lay out the fence," "Dig postholes," and "Set concrete" (with dates, of course), but

don't forget the "soft" tasks that are equally important. Your list should include items such as:

- Get building permit and schedule inspections.
- Modify plan for codes.
- Organize materials and set up workstation.
- Get helpers.

Then set up your workstation and keep clamps handy so the boards won't move around when you're cutting. If you have miter saw cuts to make, mount the saw on the work surface. Get a magnetic drill holder or quick-change sleeve. It will save hours in changing bits in your cordless drill. Metal or homemade wood guides will speed accurate cutting. You'll also want to keep the work site orderly. Nothing beats getting to work each day without having to hunt for tools or materials.

VERTICAL BOARD FENCES

Vertical board fences are probably the most prevalent style of fence constructed. That's because they go up easily, and you can vary their design almost infinitely. Styles with surface-mounted infill have only one "good" side, so you'll have to decide whether it's you or the neighbors who will look at the frame. Installing inset infill makes a fence look the same from both sides.

A solid board fence, with no gaps between the boards, can create a fully enclosed, very private space. It can also feel confining. Consider alternating the height of the bays or adding a lattice top panel to add variety and open up the view. Or you can alternate boards with slats—1×6s with 1×2s—and leave spaces between them. This design looks refined and adds an interesting play of light and shadow.

Whatever fence style you choose, first decide how wide you want the bays to be. Then divide that measurement by the width of the boards (or the boards and spaces) to choose the infill you want.

Vertical board fences usually reach 6 feet— higher, if necessary, and where codes permit.

▲ Solid board fencing without slats can provide complete privacy. This dog-eared 6-foot solid board fence protects the interior garden. Add visual interest by alternating board sizes.

SOLID BOARD FENCE

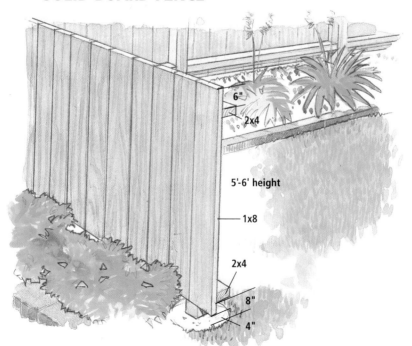

6"

2x4

5'-6' height

1x8

2x4

8"

4"

◄ One-by-six or 1x8 infill boards are used for solid board fencing (home centers offer precut panels). Add interest and style by cutting a pattern at the top or install a lattice top panel.

1 Lay out and set posts for 6- to 8-foot bays. Then build a flat-rail frame (page 134) or an edge-rail frame (page 132) with the rails flush with the posts. On longer bays, you may want to add a center rail to help keep the infill from sagging. Toenail the rails to the posts.

2 Use 1×6 or 1×8 infill boards for a solid fence and cut a pattern for the top if desired. Make your pattern cutting easier by clamping three boards together and cutting the pattern all at once. As an alternative, you can buy precut panels at your home center.

3 Starting at an end post or a gate post, fasten the infill to the rails with 2-inch coated screws. Fasten the top of the board first, plumb it with a carpenter's level, then fasten the bottom of the board.

HOW TO USE
VERTICAL BOARD FENCES

- **Defining spaces:** Very good, but can seem imposing.
- **Security:** Excellent, especially with heights of more than 6 feet.
- **Privacy:** Good; closed styles can provide considerable privacy.
- **Creating comfort zones:** Fair; blocks sun but can force wind into downdrafts.

4 Measure the opening for the gate and construct the gate using the techniques shown on page 82. Mark the position of the hinges on the gate frame and fasten the hinges with coated screws.

5 If the gate is small enough, hanging it may be a one-person job. Use blocks to support it (see page 90). For larger gates enlist the aid of a helper. Fasten the top hinge first. Then line up the bottom hinge and mark its position on the post. Pull the hinge pin if the hinge style permits it and install the hinge plate. Fasten the middle hinge last. Mark the position of the latch hardware and install it.

BOARD AND BATTENS

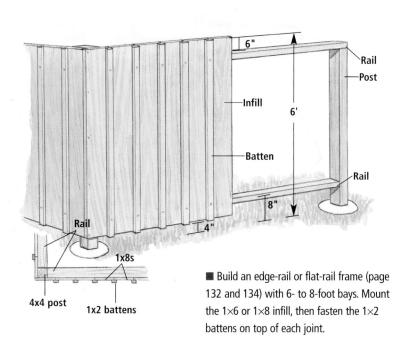

Rail
Post
Infill
Batten
Rail
6"
6'
8"
4"
Rail
1x8s
4x4 post
1x2 battens

A board-and-batten fence is a variation of the vertical board style, but with the three-dimensional addition of battens on the surface.

The battens (generally 1×2s) help break up the expanse of the fence and add a small amount of texture that has a large impact on the way the fence looks. Board-and-batten construction is time-consuming and costly, but the aesthetic return is high, making this fence and the effort to build it a worthwhile investment.

■ Build an edge-rail or flat-rail frame (page 132 and 134) with 6- to 8-foot bays. Mount the 1×6 or 1×8 infill, then fasten the 1×2 battens on top of each joint.

BOARD-ON-BOARD FENCE

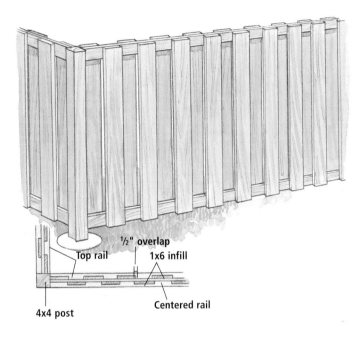

½" overlap
Top rail   1x6 infill

4x4 post   Centered rail

■ Depending on how much you overlap the boards, a board-on-board fence creates full or partial privacy. No matter what the spacing, this fence will protect you from the wind, breaking it up into little breezes.

In the style shown here, the infill is fastened to either side of centered edge rails. That creates a fence that looks good from both sides.

Surface-mounted infill is easier to install but leaves more open space between the sides, decreasing the gracefulness inherent in this style.

1 Build an edge-rail frame with 6- to 8-foot bays, centering the rails on the posts (add a flat rail at the bottom if your design calls for it). Starting at an end post, fasten 1×6 infill to one side of the fence, using a hanging spacer to keep the boards at consistent intervals. Fasten the top of the infill first, plumb the board, then fasten the bottom.

2 Start the infill on the other side of the fence, overlapping the boards on the first side of the fence by ½ inch. Using the same techniques and the spacer, fasten the infill to the second side. The spacer will keep the boards overlapped consistently. Top off the fence with a top rail and a 2×6 cap rail if desired.

Horizontal rail fences come in a variety of styles, but all of them bring a simple, modest beauty to a landscape. Capped post-and-rail fences, an outgrowth of earlier styles, go well in contemporary settings. Close rail spacing increases privacy, alternate widths add interest, and the cap rail strengthens the structure. Notched post-and-rail fences bring a classic ranch look that feels at home in many landscape styles. Rustic mortised fences (see page 36), usually with only two or three rails, are also adaptable to almost any landscape theme.

Material costs for a capped post-and-rail fence will run on the high side because of the large quantity of lumber required. Notched and mortised fences are less expensive, but require more assembly time.

When constructing a capped or notched fence, always offset the rail joints on alternate courses and prefinish the fence before assembling it to make sure all surfaces are protected from the elements.

HOW TO USE
HORIZONTAL RAIL FENCES

- **Defining spaces:** Excellent; they make attractive boundary markers.
- **Security:** Poor; low fences are easy to climb over.
- **Privacy:** None; open rails permit open views.
- **Creating comfort zones:** Minimal; low height does not block wind. Closely spaced rails can block drifting snow.

CAPPED POST-AND-RAIL FENCE

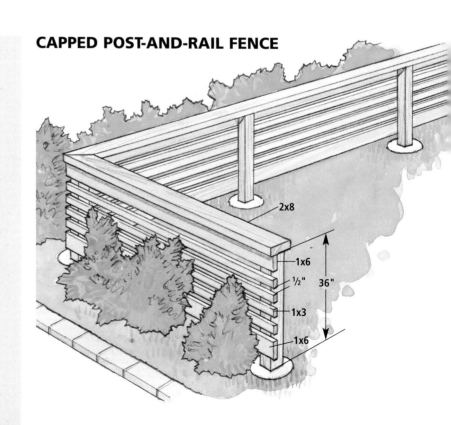

2x8

1x6

½"

36"

1x3

1x6

1 Lay out your fence line and set posts for 4- to 6-foot bays. Cut the posts level with each other. Using a combination square, mark the center of the posts. You can mark only the locations where the rails will fall or scribe the line down the length of the post. The line will ensure that you have jointed rails centered.

2 Starting at the top, fasten the first rail flush with the top of the posts. Then alternate 1×6s and 1×3s, spacing them with a 2×2 spacer. Note that butted rails alternate with through rails every other board. Staggering the joints in this fashion increases the strength of the fence.

Drive angled screws to keep the mitered corner tight

3 Measure and cut a 2×8 top rail, mitering the corners. Cut the miter first, then cut the other end of the rail so that any joint will be centered on a post. Apply a thin bead of clear silicone caulk to the edges of the mitered corners, then fasten the rail to the posts. Pull the mitered edges together with angled screws. Wipe off any excess caulk with a damp rag.

NOTCHED POST-AND-RAIL FENCE

36" to 48"

Notched post-and-rail fences take a little more time to install than other fences. In part this is because of the time it takes to cut the notches, but also because you must level and set each bay individually. That way you are assured that the notches will be level with each other. The proportions of the fence will differ with its size and bay width. For a 4-foot fence, fasten 1×4 rails to 4×4 posts, 6 to 8 feet apart. For a 5-foot fence, use 6×6 posts with 2×6s for rails. Buy 16-foot rails so you can span two 8-foot sections, but be sure to offset the joints on alternate courses. Surface-mounted rails go up faster but are structurally weaker and less attractive, even with staggered joints.

1 Cut your posts to a length that will allow you to set them deep enough for local code compliance and still leave 36 inches above ground. Clamp them together with pipe clamps, keeping the tops flush with each other. Mark the position of the notches on the end posts and snap chalk lines across all the faces. Cut and chisel the notches (see page 136). Then cut the rails and prefinish them if desired.

4' level

2x4 temporary crosspiece

2x4 braces on each side keep top of post 36" off the ground.

2 Lay out your fence line, dig the holes, and set the posts in loosely (but not in concrete). Hold the first post plumb and fasten 2×4 braces at its base so the top of the post is 36 inches off the ground. Backfill the post hole with concrete, plumb the post, and let the concrete set up (it doesn't have to cure). Then hold the second post upright and insert a 2×4 in the notches of both posts. Level the 2×4 and fasten 2×4 bottom braces to the second post. Backfill the second posthole and let the concrete set. Repeat the process for all posts and let the concrete cure.

Butted rail

Through rail

3 Distribute the rails along the fence line so they will be close at hand when you need them. Insert the rails in the notches, centering any joints on the post, and fasten the rails with coated screws. Note that butted rails should alternate with through rails to add strength to the fence.

BASKET-WEAVE FENCES

Basket-weave fencing gives you an opportunity to create style with little effort. It is not an inexpensive fence (especially with special-ordered infill), but it creates interesting shadow lines, admits breezes, and maintains privacy. Choose the infill width carefully. Over a long fence line, wide infill boards (1×8s) can begin to look pretty overwhelming. Narrower boards (down to 1×4s) will add interest to the architecture of the fence and make it seem less imposing. Because weave itself adds strength to the frame, you may not need a kickboard for rail support, but you can add one for appearance, of course.

A 1×3 (or 1×2) spacer creates a center point around which the infill is woven. Benderboard, commonly ½×4 or ½×6, is often used in basket-weave designs, but ⅜-inch redwood is better. It stands up to the elements, imparts a strong,

warm feeling to the design, and is much easier to install than thicker stock. You'll spend more time building a basket-weave fence than a fence with surface-mounted infill, but less time than louvered or other fences with inset infill.

BASKET-WEAVE FENCE

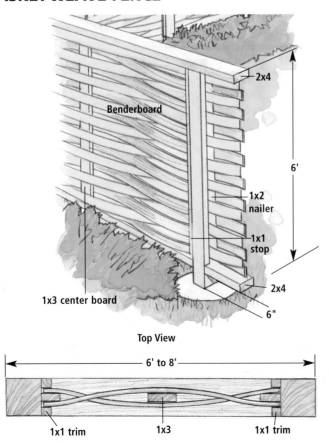

Benderboard

2x4

Benderboard

6'

1x2 nailer

1x1 stop

1x3 center board

2x4

6"

Top View

6' to 8'

1x1 trim   1x3   1x1 trim

HOW TO USE
BASKET-WEAVE FENCES

■ **Defining spaces:** Excellent; but can dominate small areas.

■ **Security:** Poor; the weave makes the fence easy to climb.

■ **Privacy:** Very good; even though the weave is open, you can't see directly through it.

■ **Creating comfort zones:** Good; softens winds and blocks sunlight.

① Lay out the fence line and set posts for 6- to 8-foot (maximum) bays. Build a flat-rail frame (page 134), measure the space between the top and bottom rail, and fasten the 1×3 center board in each bay.

② At each post measure the space between the top and bottom rails (they might be slightly different in each bay) and cut 1×2 or 1×3 stops to fit. Mark the center of all the posts and fasten the stop to the posts with finishing nails.

③ With a helper holding one end of an infill slat snugly against the stop on one post, wind the other end behind the stop on the opposite post and mark its length. Cut all the infill slats for the bay to this length. Fasten the slat to the stops at each end with #8 2-inch coated screws, or 6d or 8d box nails (angle them into the post faces). Then fasten the slat to the centerboard. Weave and fasten the next slat from the opposite side and continue hanging the infill until you have filled the frame. Then trim out the ends of the slats with 1×1 trim. Repeat the process for the remaining bays.

LOUVERED FENCES

A louvered fence imparts a lot of textural interest to any landscape. What's more, it will increase privacy without restricting summer breezes, filter the sunlight through a garden bed planted in its shadow, and add security to a pool or patio.

Louvers splash light and shadow across the surface of a fence line. They produce partial privacy by limiting the outside view to only a portion of the yard at a time. But depending on their angle, that privacy can "disappear" if the viewer is moving at even a slow rate of speed past the fence (for example, traveling in a car past a front-yard louvered fence).

Louvers should be built with kiln-dried lumber to minimize warping and with a kickboard so the weight of the louvers won't sag the rails. You can set 1×6 louvers on a 2×4 frame as shown here, or rip 1×6s to fit. You can also use 1×4s on a 2×4 frame or 1×6s on a 2×6 frame, centering the louvers inside the edges of the rails. The 1$^{15}/_{16}$-inch spacer shown will allow an even number of louvers to fit inside a 6-, 7-, or 8-foot frame. The 2⅜-inch spacers will not quite fill a bay evenly and will leave a gap at both ends, but you can fill the gap with thin stock. Draw out your pattern on ½-inch graph paper (to actual size) before you buy materials.

LOUVERED FENCE

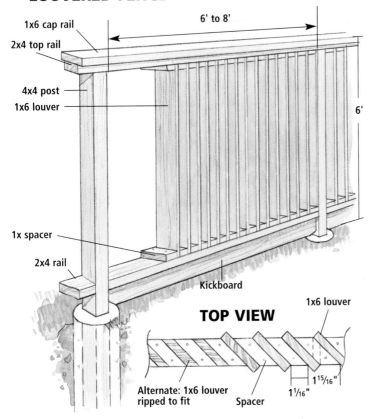

- 1x6 cap rail
- 2x4 top rail
- 6' to 8'
- 4x4 post
- 1x6 louver
- 6'
- 1x spacer
- 2x4 rail
- Kickboard

TOP VIEW

- 1x6 louver
- Alternate: 1x6 louver ripped to fit
- Spacer
- 1$^{1}/_{16}$"
- 1$^{15}/_{16}$"

HOW TO USE
LOUVERED FENCES

- **Defining spaces:** Excellent; they make friendly fence boundary markers.
- **Security:** Very good; sturdy and hard to climb from either side.
- **Privacy:** Moderate; some visibility is possible from outside.
- **Creating comfort zones:** Good; louvers redirect winds and filter sunlight. Featherboard does not make a good windscreen—the wind will vault it.

① Lay out your fence line with 6- to 8-foot bays, dig the holes, and set the posts. Build a flat-rail frame (page 134) and cut the louvers to fit between the rails. If you're using 1×6 louvers, set them at 45 degrees with a combination square, centering it on the rail. If you're using 1×6 louvers, position the first louver with one corner against the post and the opposite lined up with the edge of the rail (see illustration, opposite). Toenail the louver to the bottom rail, plumb it, and attach it with screws driven through the top rail.

② Cut and install spacers, fastening them to the top and bottom rail. As an alternative, you can tack a spacer to the rails, install the louver, and remove and reuse the spacer.

③ Continue installing alternate louvers and spacers until you fill the bay. Top off the fence with a 2×6 or 2×8 cap rail.

FEATHERBOARD FENCE

A featherboard fence is a closed louvered fence. The closed surface gives you maximum privacy with attractive shadows where the boards overlap. Build a flat-rail frame and fasten a set of 1×1 stops to the rails. Toenail the infill (1×4s or 1×6s) to the rails, and when all the infill is mounted, fasten 1×1 stops on the other side.

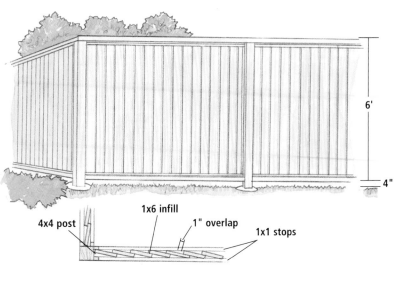

6'

4"

4x4 post

1x6 infill

1" overlap

1x1 stops

MORTISED POST-AND-RAIL FENCES

1 Lay out the fence line with 6-foot bays and dig the holes. Cut the posts to a length that will let you set them deep enough for code compliance and still leave 36 inches above ground. Cut a cardboard rectangle the size of the tenon and use it as a template to outline the mortise on the posts. Measure down from the top of the post the same distance so the mortises will all be on the same plane. Drill and chisel out the mortise.

Building suppliers sell rustic rails with wedge-shaped, tapered, or rounded tenons and premortised posts. They're ready for installation, but you can also cut your own traditional rails from raw logs. If you start from scratch, the rustic look allows you a certain amount of leeway and is forgiving of minor mistakes.

Precut rails come in lengths of 6 to 10 feet and may be square (sawn rails) or wedge-shaped (split). These fences tend to look more stylish with shorter bays, but a 10-foot rail covers more fence line with fewer posts (and fewer precut tenons) and is therefore less expensive. If cost is a factor, you may want to strike a balance between the two lengths.

The standard length for split, wedge-shaped cedar, pine, or redwood rails with 4- or 6-inch faces is 6 to 11 feet. If you're cutting your own, you'll have a good deal of flexibility in how wide you make the bays.

Measure down from the top of the post to mark each mortise location so the mortises are in the same place on all posts. You should be able to locate the top rail 2 to 6 inches from the top of the post and the bottom rail 6 to 12 inches off the ground, with the middle rail centered between them. You must set mortised fences one section at a time—the rails will not fit in preset posts.

HOW TO USE
MORTISED POST-AND-RAIL FENCES

■ **Defining spaces:** Excellent; they make attractive boundary markers.

■ **Security:** Poor; low fences are easy to climb over.

■ **Privacy:** None; open rails permit open views.

■ **Creating comfort zones:** Minimal; low height does not block wind. With closely spaced rails, they can block drifting snow.

2 Position the cardboard template on the end of the rails and outline the profile of the tenon with a carpenter's pencil. Mark the depth of the tenon on the side of the rails and use a reciprocating saw to rough-cut the tenons. You can narrow their ends and fine-tune them to fit when you install the rails.

3 Set the first post in its hole and brace it 36 inches off the ground using the same techniques shown for a notched fence (pages 30–31). Test-fit the tenons in this post and the next one, shave them to fit, and set them aside. Backfill the first hole with concrete and let it set. Then set the rails in the next post, brace and plumb it with level rails, and backfill the hole with concrete.

4 Continue setting each bay with the same techniques, leveling the rails and backfilling the holes with concrete.

RUSTIC MORTISE STYLES

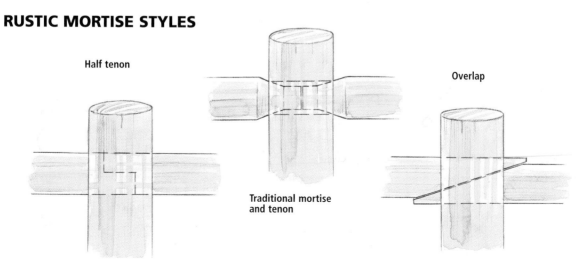

Half tenon

Traditional mortise and tenon

Overlap

PICKET FENCES

P icket fences are probably the most timeless and universal design of all fence styles. They look equally stylish in a wide variety of landscapes, from Victorian to modern themes, augmenting the appeal of any landscape theme with their innate beauty.

Before you choose your picket style, take a tour through your home center. One of the items you'll find is preassembled 8-foot panels ready for installation, but if you decide to save yourself some time with this kind of product, make sure it's durable. Look for high-quality lumber (few knots and smooth finishes) and be wary of stapled frames. Cabinet shops will mill special orders and a lumberyard might cut pickets for you for a fee—and of course you can cut your own designs too.

It doesn't matter whether you install the pickets on flush edge-rail or flat-rail frames, but if you like the looks of a flat-rail fence, you should add a kickboard to your design to minimize sagging. Most picket fences are installed on 4×4 posts and look best between

Batten keeps pickets lined up.

1 Lay out the fence line with 6- to 8-foot bays, dig the holes, and set the posts with their tops 36 to 48 inches above the ground. Build edge-rail frames between the posts. Tack a batten 2 to 4 inches above the ground and use it to keep the bottom of the pickets on the same plane when you fasten them. Measure the distance between posts to compute the number of pickets you'll need to fill the bay. Recheck your measurements after installing the first few pickets and adjust the spacing if necessary.

36 and 48 inches tall. Use 6×6 posts for fences taller than 5 feet (taller than this, and the fence starts looking like a stockade).

Before you put up a picket fence, experiment with picket widths and spacing to get the look you want. Traditional 1×3 or 1×4 pickets spaced 2½ to 3 inches apart will give you a classic look, but there's a lot of leeway within those guidelines. To experiment with the possibilities, draw your ideas to scale on ¼-inch graph paper.

First establish your bay width–6 to 8 feet is ideal. Then, to figure the picket spacing, decide how many pickets you want to spread across the bay. Multiply that number by the actual picket width and subtract the result from the bay width to find the total amount of open space. Divide this figure by a number one more than the number of pickets to find the distance between them.

2 Distribute your pickets along the bay so they will be handy when you need them. Using the results of your computation for the number and spacing of the pickets, make a cleated spacer as shown above. Set each picket on the batten, space it with the spacer, and fasten it to the rails.

HOW TO USE
PICKET FENCES

- **Defining spaces:** Excellent; they clearly define any boundary with classic style.
- **Security:** Moderate; they keep children and pets in or out, and pointed pickets can make it difficult to hop over.
- **Privacy:** None; open picket design permits open views.
- **Creating comfort zones:** Minimal; low height does not block wind, but closely spaced pickets can block drifting snow.

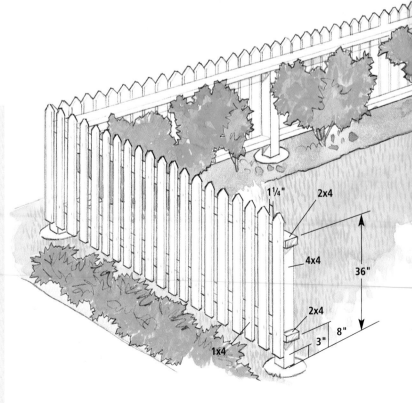

▲ Pickets typically are spaced 2½ to 3 inches apart. This traditional picket fence is unassuming, yet provides an attractive border and protects the surrounding landscape.

CUTTING YOUR OWN DESIGN

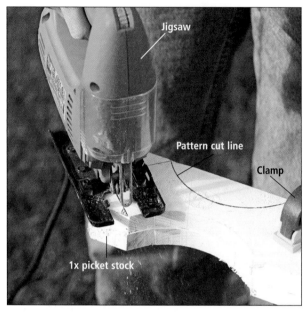

Jigsaw

Pattern cut line

Clamp

1x picket stock

You can customize the style of your pickets for a one-of-a-kind fence line. All you need is a little time, a dash of creativity, and a jigsaw. Experiment on paper with the pattern until you like the result. Then outline the pattern on a cardboard template and use the template to transfer the pattern to the 1× picket stock. Clamp two to four pickets together and cut the pattern with a jigsaw. Smooth the cut with 80-grit sandpaper.

▶ Picket fencing does not have to be white, nor does it have to cut from the same picket design. These pickets are patterned and installed to form a unique design.

▲ This white picket fence is clean and simple. The slightly scalloped gate flanked by finials adds visual interest and is the perfect entrance to the curved walkway.

▲ A lush garden and flowering annuals teamed with a white picket fence creates a cottage style look.

SCALLOPING YOUR PICKET FENCE

A scalloped fence usually looks better with pickets spaced closer than the traditional 2½ to 3 inches. Start experimenting on paper with your own design by spacing them about half a picket width apart.

Lay out the curve with a length of heavy (but flexible) rope or decorator's cord about 2 feet longer than the span. Tack one end of the rope to the center of the picket or post at which the scallop will begin. Drape the other end over a nail at the opposite end of the scallop. Move the free end of the rope to adjust the curve, and when it's right (at least 1½ inches above the rail), tack the free end with another nail. Tape the rope in place and pencil the curve on the face of the pickets (use a carpenter's pencil). Mark the ends of the curve on the rope so you can duplicate the curve and remove the rope. Cut the pickets along the line with a jigsaw and sand the tops smooth.

SIDING FENCES

▶ Siding fences are best for matching the architectural design of the home. The same siding used on the home can be used on the fence—one or both sides of the fence can be covered. These wood shingles provide complete privacy and the hollow core helps control noise.

If you're looking for a way to integrate the architectural style of your house with other elements in the landscape, consider a siding fence. These fences allow you to duplicate exactly a number of different materials used on the surface of homes. Even if your house is finished with masonry or brick, a siding fence makes an architectural statement. Siding fences can provide total privacy if built tall enough, and those styles built with hollow cores, such as shingle and clapboard, are best for noise control.

Hollow-core fences need a reinforced frame. Standard 2×4s are OK (so are 2×6s), but you'll need studs to provide additional support as well as a nailing surface for some materials.

On the whole, siding fences cost more than other kinds of fencing. For example, tongue-and-groove lumber, like any other milled stock, is expensive. But if you're planning to paint your fence, you can save money by buying finger-jointed tongue-and-groove stock. Finger-jointed millwork is made from shorter pieces joined with glued finger joints. It's strong, but needs protection from the elements–finish it with high-quality primer and alkyd paint. Clapboard siding is more reasonably priced and construction will go quickly. Plywood, once fairly inexpensive, has risen in price, but building a plywood fence is an easy task.

For most styles, start construction of a siding fence by setting your posts at least 3 feet in the ground (or to the depth required by local codes). Don't be concerned with aesthetics when spacing your posts; they are less visible in this design. Post spacing of 8 feet will work well with most materials.

Next build a flat-rail frame (see page 134) and, if required by the fence style, toenail 2×4 studs to the top and bottom rails every 16 inches. Use pressure-treated lumber

1 Lay out your fence line for 8-foot bays, dig the postholes and set the posts. Build a flat-rail frame with a third rail if you plan to make a double-paneled fence as illustrated (opposite). Mark the position of the first stops on one side of the rails and posts, using a reveal that will center the panel in the frame. Nail the stops to one side of the frame. Cut the panel stock to fit the interior dimensions of the frame and toenail it to the rails and posts.

throughout the frame—the cavity between the exterior and interior faces will trap moisture so you need rot-resistant framing. When installing any panel materials, use the methods for a plywood fence. Toenail lattice into the rails between 1× stops. For acrylic panel, precaulk the rail along the stop with silicone. In most settings and with most materials, a 1×8 cap rail enhances the appearance of a siding fence.

Plywood

A solid-panel plywood fence can look stylish despite the simplicity of its

How to Use
Siding Fences

■ **Defining spaces:** Excellent; they make very attractive dividers, but will look imposing on a long fence line and will overwhelm a small space.

■ **Security:** Excellent; but only if the fence is high, which may mar the overall appearance of the fence. Impenetrable and difficult to climb.

■ **Privacy:** Excellent; tall fences offer total privacy.

■ **Creating comfort zones:** Moderate; blocks noise, sun, and snow. Not a good windbreak—it's not tall enough and the wind will vault over a solid structure.

2 When you have fastened the panel to the frame, measure and cut the trim to fit, mitering the corners. Install the trim against the panel with finishing nails. Use the same techniques to finish the remainder of the fence. Install a 1×6 cap rail, mitering the corner.

SHINGLE FENCE

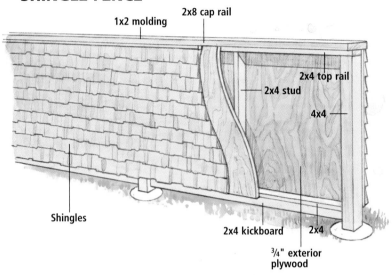

1x2 molding
2x8 cap rail
2x4 top rail
2x4 stud
4x4
Shingles
2x4 kickboard
2x4
¾" exterior plywood

▲ Lay out the fence line for 8-foot bays, dig the holes, and set the posts. Build a flat-rail frame with a kickboard, fastening a 2×4 stud in the center of each bay. Fasten ¾-inch exterior-grade plywood to both sides of the frames, flush with the top of the top rail. Working from the bottom up, install cedar shingles. Finish the fence with a 2×8 cap rail.

TONGUE-AND-GROOVE SIDING

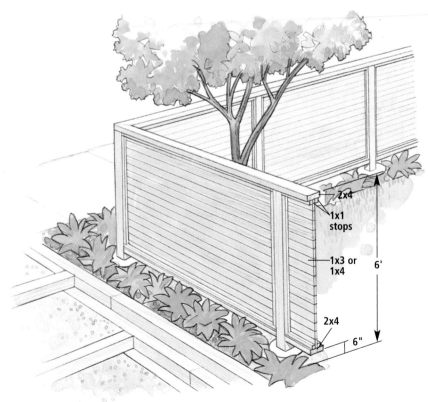

2x4
1x1 stops
1x3 or 1x4
6'
2x4
6"

construction. Because plywood comes in 4×8 sheets, fence designs with 4- or 8-foot bays will reduce or eliminate cutting the panels, and construction will go faster.

Only exterior-grade plywood will withstand the elements. Use ⅝- or ¾-inch sheets. They will provide the structural support required and will resist bowing in heavy winds.

Textured plywood siding is a good choice for fences too. It comes in several patterns. Simplify finishing tasks by using primed or prestained material.

Shingles

The highly textured surface of wood shingles gives a fence a rich and warm appearance. Shingles are sold by the bundle and vary in cost according to the grade. Relatively inexpensive No. 3 shingles have some

◄ Lay out the fence line for 8-foot bays, dig the holes, and set the posts. Build a flat-rail frame in each bay. Cut 1× stops and install them on the rails and posts. Then cut tongue-and-groove stock to fit the bay. Starting at the bottom, toenail the infill to the posts, tongue-side up. Run a bead of polyurethane glue on the tongue of each board before fastening the next one. Continue until the bay is filled. Then install the stops on the other side.

knots and are specified for walls. No. 1 shingles are made for roofs and will cost much more. Cover the frame with ¾-inch plywood sheathing or nail 1×4 horizontal furring strips to the studs, spacing them at the length of the shingles (generally 15 to 18 inches). Fasten the shingles with 3d galvanized or aluminum box nails (two per shingle, ¾ inch from edges). Space the shingles ⅛ inch apart and stagger the overlaps 1½ inches. To keep the courses straight, snap a chalk line across each row at the point where the next course will begin.

Tongue and groove

Because its edges interlock, tongue-and-groove siding creates an extremely solid fence with a style that will suit almost any location. Shadow lines at the joints interrupt the surface with a subtle rhythm. The fence has an ordered, elegant overall appearance.

Clapboard

Nail a starter strip (as thick as the bottom edge of the siding) along the bottom of the frame. Then, working upwards, fasten the siding to the posts and studs with 8d galvanized nails. If you're not going to paint the fence, use aluminum siding nails.

Other materials

For siding with a rabbeted bottom edge (Dolly Varden), beveled siding, or shiplap siding, install the infill without a starter strip. Attach these materials with 8d casing nails.

CLAPBOARD SIDING

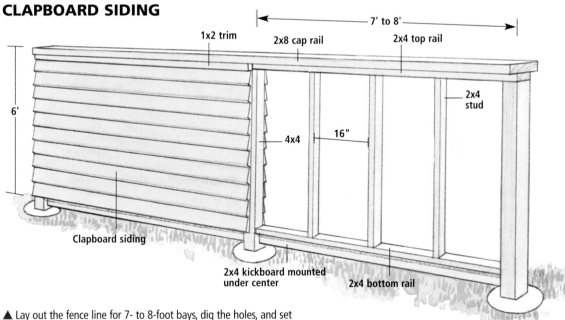

▲ Lay out the fence line for 7- to 8-foot bays, dig the holes, and set the posts. Build a flat-rail frame in each bay with a 2×4 kickboard and studs. Cut clapboard siding to length and install it on one side of the fence. Work from the bottom up and offset the joints on the center of the studs and rails. Repeat for the other side and finish the fence with a 2×8 cap rail.

Lattice Fences

Latticework, with its thin, crisscrossed wood slats, has been around for more than 2,000 years, and it's no wonder. It's lightweight, multifunctional, and the play of light and shadow over its surface is irresistible to the eye. Vines and climbing plants consider it "home," and its open surface lets in light and smooths out the wind.

Prefabricated 4×8 wood or vinyl panels (with diagonal or rectangular grids) are available at building-supply outlets and lumberyards. And with a little time and patience, you can make your own lattice (see page 120). Wood lattice comes in several thicknesses. Use a lattice that's at least ¾ inch thick (at the intersection of the

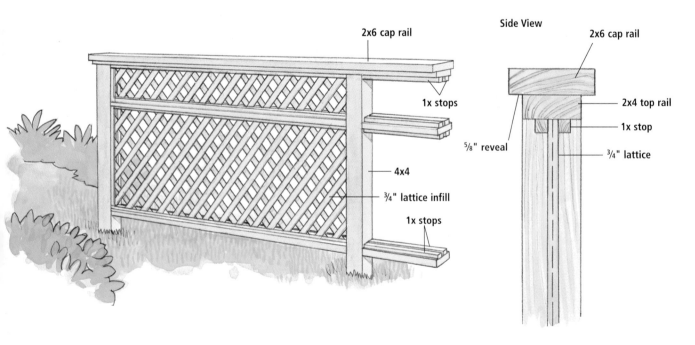

2x6 cap rail

1x stops

4x4

¾" lattice infill

1x stops

Side View

2x6 cap rail

2x4 top rail

1x stop

⅝" reveal

¾" lattice

boards). The thicker pieces resist warping and cracking, reducing future maintenance—a good return on its slightly higher cost. Lattice goes up easiest and looks best inset in the frame. You can set it between stops as shown here or into dadoes cut vertically in the fence frame.

HOW TO USE
LATTICE FENCES

- **Defining spaces:** Excellent; makes a neighbor-friendly, attractive boundary marker.
- **Security:** Minimal; lattice is easily broken.
- **Privacy:** Good; the fence pattern, not the view behind it, holds the eye.
- **Creating comfort zones:** Good; softens winds and filters sunlight.

1 Lay out your fence line for 6- to 8-foot bays, dig the holes, and set and cut the posts. Install a flat-rail frame (page 134), adding rails to separate one panel from another. Mark the position of the rails on the posts (measuring from the top of the post down) and toenail the rails in place.

DESIGNING WITH LATTICE

If you haven't looked closely, you may not have noticed that all latticework is not created equal. Not only is lattice manufactured from a variety of materials, the materials have various textures, and the lattice openings themselves vary in size depending on their intended use.

The toughest lattice is made with cedar 1×2s (¾ inch thick, 1½ inches wide). Technically this stock is neither lath nor strips. It lasts forever, will hold heavy vines without sagging, and should be used in large lattice screens, trellises, and arbors. Thinner lattice may prove to be an immediate disappointment in these structures.

Standard lattice comes in thicknesses from ½ inch to 1 inch at the intersection of the boards. Garden lattice spacing is 2⅝ inches wide. If you want a privacy screen, get lattice with privacy spacing— from ¾ to 1¾ inches wide.

2 Add the thickness of the lattice and the inside and outside stops; then subtract the result from the width of the rails. Divide this result by 2. This is the amount of reveal—the space between the edge of the rail and the edge of the stop. Mark the posts and rails at this width, cut the rail stock to fit the frame, and fasten it to the rails and posts with finishing nails. Cut and miter the stops, predrill them, and push the nails into the holes. This will make it easier to keep the stops lined up as you fasten them.

3 To fasten any panel material, including lattice, tongue-and-groove stock, or plywood, cut the material to fit the opening of the frame, and toenail it to the rails—not the stops. Set the bottom panel material in the frame first, then the top.

4 Cut the lattice panel for the top section to fit the frame and secure it to the rails and posts with finishing nails.

5 Cut the other set of 1× stops and miter them (if you have not done so already). Fasten them snug against the lattice panel.

INSTALLING LATTICE ON 6×6 POSTS

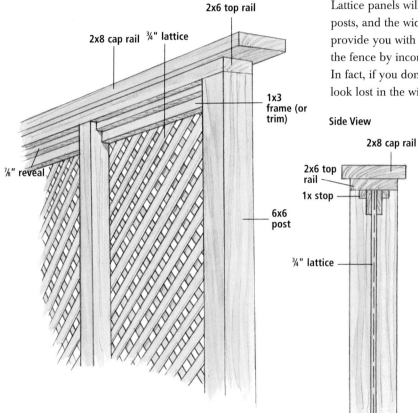

2x6 top rail

2x8 cap rail

¾" lattice

1x3 frame (or trim)

⅞" reveal

Side View

2x8 cap rail

2x6 top rail

1x stop

¾" lattice

6x6 post

Lattice panels will work equally well on 4×4 and 6×6 posts, and the wider surface of the larger posts will provide you with an opportunity to enhance the style of the fence by incorporating additional trim into the design. In fact, if you don't add the trim, the lattice will tend to look lost in the wider frame.

Because the lattice is ¾ inch thick and the post is 5½ inches wide, you have 4½ inches of post face to play with (or 2⅜ inches on each side of the lattice. The illustration (left) shows one way of trimming out the wide posts—with 1× stock ripped to various widths, each layer creating repeated reveals. Such small details add interest to the fence at very little cost.

Experiment with your own design on graph paper before buying materials. You can build the lattice in trimmed frames first (page 120) and install the frames between stops. Or you can use the same construction methods used for a 2×4 frame, installing one set of stops, then the lattice, then the other set of stops.

INSTALLING VINYL LATTICE

Vinyl lattice comes in a number of colors, and some styles are molded with a woodgrain look-alike pattern. Installation of vinyl fence panels relies on the same methods used for wood lattice—fastening the panel between two sets of 1× stops on the rails and posts. Vinyl lattice is not as stiff as wood lattice, however, so the ends will tend to flop when you cut it. To stabilize the lattice, clamp two pieces of 1× stock along the cut line and cut it with a fine-toothed handsaw, jigsaw, or circular saw.

INSTALLING A PREFABRICATED PANEL FENCE

P refabricated fence panels come already assembled—all you have to do is lay out the fence line, set the posts, and hang the panels, of course. These panels take care of all the measuring and cutting chores. They're made for quick construction.

Once available in only one or two styles, you'll now find lattice infill, lattice on tongue-and-groove, offset board-on-board, dog-eared, and picket-shaped infill. With this many (and more) styles, you won't have any trouble finding something to match your tastes as well as your time. Look for well-made panels—they might cost a little more, but they'll pay off in the long run. If your kit doesn't come with decorative post caps, you can pick them up at your home center or chamfer the posts to help shed water.

1 Following the manufacturer's instructions, lay out and set the posts with the specified spacing. Let the concrete cure. Before installing each panel, test-fit it between the posts. It should fit snugly. If it's slightly undersize that's OK, but if it isn't wide enough to hang in the brackets, add trim stock to the edges. Trim oversize panels on both sides with a circular saw.

2 Mark the position of the brackets on the posts as specified by the manufacturer and fasten the brackets to the posts. Use special care when driving bracket nails with a hammer so you don't bend the bracket. Driving screws with a cordless drill is "safer."

3 Hanging prefab panels is a two-person job. Raise the panel above the top bracket and slide it down through the center brackets until it rests in the flange of the bottom bracket.

4 Install the gate with the hardware provided by the manufacturer or use the hardware of your choice, making sure your own hardware meets the same specifications as the hinges in the kit. Mark the end posts for the height and snap a chalk line between them to mark the intermediate posts. Use a reciprocating saw to cut the posts.

HOW TO USE
PREFAB PANEL FENCES

- **Defining spaces:** Good; neighbor-friendly models make attractive boundary markers.
- **Security:** Board fences make good security structures; lattice panels do not.
- **Privacy:** Good; solid boards block views. Board-on-board and lattice distract the eye.
- **Creating comfort zones:** Good; solid panels cast shadows and vault the wind. Open structures filter breezes.

ORNAMENTAL METAL FENCES

W ith the exception of customized wrought-iron fencing available from specialty manufacturers, the metal-fencing market is now almost completely occupied by tubular steel and aluminum products. These fences are available in many styles (often mimicking classic wrought-iron designs) and prices, and high-quality models are virtually maintenance free.

Tubular metal fences offer an attractive alternative to forged iron. In the right setting, they look sophisticated and ornate—from a distance, some even look like ornamental iron.

Most installation packages include assembled infill sections (in 4- to 8-foot widths), posts, flanges, and the fittings to put them all together. Some systems are designed to accept rails in holes punched in the posts. Others are fixed with brackets mounted to the posts—a stronger method of mounting. Preassembled panels require bay-by-bay installation and setting of posts. Order the material and wait for delivery before you begin laying out your fence line.

If you need to shorten a section to fit a narrow area, cut the infill first. Then cut the rails to length, making sure you have the same amount of material on both ends of the panel.

If you're fencing a steep slope, you'll need to make sure the style you're purchasing can be forced (racked) to follow the slope. Most styles are made for level ground, although you can install straight sections in a step-down design.

① Lay out the fence line, spacing the post holes as specified by the manufacturer. Set the first post in concrete, bracing it plumb and at the correct height with 2×4s, using duct tape to keep from marring the surface of the posts.

HOW TO USE
ORNAMENTAL METAL FENCES

- **Defining spaces:** Excellent. These fences set boundaries in style.
- **Security:** Very good if the fence is high enough and the infill spacing is narrow.
- **Privacy:** Poor; open infill provides very little privacy.
- **Creating comfort zones:** Poor; open infill does not filter wind or sunlight.

2 Slide the formed end of the rails into the holes in the posts. You may have to "jockey" the panel a bit to get the rails to fit all at once. Have a helper hold the panel in place so the rails don't pop out.

3 Using the fasteners provided by the manufacturer, secure the rails to the posts. If you use a cordless drill to drive the screws, set the clutch to the minimum torque setting. Do not tighten the screws completely at this time.

4 While one person continues to hold the panel in place, the other person should slide the second post toward the panel, fitting the rails into the holes in this post. Fasten the rails to this post loosely. Then set and brace the second post in concrete, leveling the panel with a carpenter's level and plumbing it with a post level. Use duct tape to prevent the braces as you did for the first post. Tighten the rail screws with a screwdriver (not a cordless drill) and let the concrete set. Mount the remaining posts in the same manner.

INSTALLING METAL SECTIONS ON WOOD POSTS

1 Lay out your fence line, spacing the posts at the distance specified by the manufacturer. Dig all the holes, then set the first post in concrete, plumbing and bracing it (pages 122–127). Let the concrete set up (but it doesn't have to cure). Place the other posts in the holes, but do not set them.

2 Fasten the panel brackets to the first (and second) post, spacing them as specified by the manufacturer (see inset). Then while holding the panel in place, slide the rails into the brackets on the first post. Push the second post toward the panel so the brackets slide into the rails on this side also.

3 Continue holding the panel in place and attach the screws loosely into the brackets. If you're using a cordless drill, set the clutch to the lowest setting to avoid overdriving the screws.

Post level

4 Continuing to hold the panel in place, set and brace the second post in concrete. Level the panel with a carpenter's level; plumb the post with a post level. Tighten the rail screws with a screwdriver (not a cordless drill) and let the concrete set before mounting the next panel. Repeat this process until you have mounted the remaining panels.

VINYL AND SYNTHETIC FENCES

Fencing made from vinyl, composites, and other synthetic products installs relatively easily and is virtually maintenance free. It won't rot, rust, chip, or fade. All styles come as kits with precut parts. Most require some degree of on-site homeowner assembly, and although the basic steps for installation are generally the same (as illustrated here), each manufacturer has installation details to which you'll want to pay attention.

A few manufacturers furnish materials that require PVC cement or other adhesive for assembly. When gluing make sure the parts are clean and that you have plenty of ventilation.

As an alternative to a gravel base in postholes, you may be able to use sand. You can easily push the post base into sand, which allows water to drain away from the base. Some styles can be forced out of shape (racked) for installation on slopes.

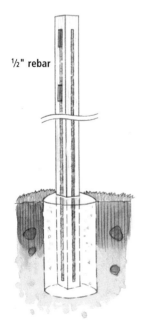

½" rebar

1 Lay out your fence line according to the manufacturer's specifications and dig all the postholes. Many vinyl fences call for end and gate posts strengthened with a concrete core. If your model requires it, insert ½-inch rebar down two opposite inside corners of the post and into the bottom of the hole. (You'll pour the concrete later.)

2 Set the first post, bracing it plumb and at the correct height as shown. Use duct tape or clamps to hold the braces on the posts. Backfill the hole with concrete and let the concrete set up (it doesn't need to cure).

3 When the concrete has set, insert the bottom rail in the holes in both the first and second post (but don't set the second post in concrete yet).

4 Assemble the panel in the manner specified by the manufacturer and install it in the bottom rail from post to post. Then push the top rail into the hole of the first post; slide it down on top of the infill and insert it into the hole in the second post.

ASSEMBLING VINYL PANELS

Assembly of the infill panels is one area in which there is a wide difference among styles and manufacturers. Some styles call for panel sections that slide together with grooved edges (above left). Others use panel sections whose edges are held together by a spline (above center). For any method that requires a "third hand" (above right), build an assembly jig from 2×4s. Fasten the 2×4 blocks to the base so the bottom rail just fits between them.

5 While a helper holds the panel in place, set the second post in concrete, plumbing it and bracing it as you did the first post. While the concrete sets up, install any fasteners required, as shown in the next two steps.

6 Different manufacturers equip their fences with different fasteners. Most will require some kind of fastener driven from inside the post at an angle into the rail. Start with the clutch of a cordless drill at the lightest setting and finish tightening with a screwdriver.

7 Using the same techniques, drive fasteners along the rail and into the infill as required.

8 Mix a batch of concrete with a pourable consistency by adding a little more water than you would for a mortar mix. Then pour concrete into the end and gate posts to within 6 inches of the top.

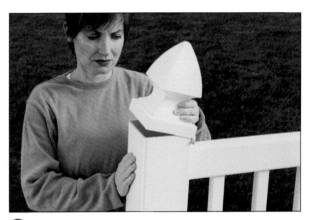

9 Attach caps to the posts using glue or screws, as required by the manufacturer.

HOW TO USE
VINYL AND SYNTHETIC FENCES

■ **Defining spaces:** Use in a setting not requiring a great deal of structural strength and where low maintenance is desirable.

■ **Security:** Characteristics vary with infill style, but synthetic fences do not provide security.

RACKING A VINYL FENCE

Some vinyl and synthetic fence styles are made with the capacity to be racked to a contour that follows a slope. Others are not intended for that purpose but can be modified. Rail-and-baluster styles are the most adaptable.

You might be able to miter the end of the rails and lengthen the punched postholes to change the angle of the frame.

Be aware, however, that the amount of adjustment you can make is likely to be small and such modifications may void the manufacturer's warranty.

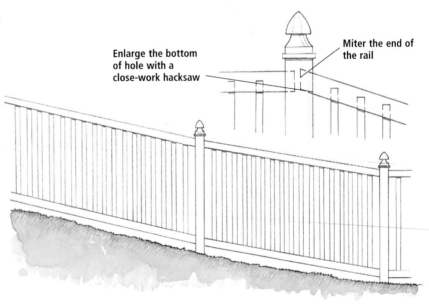

Enlarge the bottom of hole with a close-work hacksaw

Miter the end of the rail

INSTALLING A CHAIN LINK FENCE

You can hardly beat chain link for a long-lasting, almost maintenance-free fence. It is a great choice whether you need to keep kids or pets contained within a yard, to stop youngsters from wandering into a swimming pool, or just to define your property line in a no-frills, utilitarian way.

Constructing a chain link fence is not difficult. You can fence in a moderately sized yard in a couple of weekends, and you'll find all the tools at your local fence supplier.

Most residential applications will call for a 4-, 5-, or 6-foot fence. These are standard heights for chain link mesh (also called the fabric), but you can order heights to 10 feet and more. The mesh is woven from 6-gauge to 11-gauge galvanized steel (6-gauge is thicker and thus stronger), and you can also find vinyl-coated fencing in a variety of colors. Vinyl sleeves are available for the posts, so you can color coordinate your entire installation. Strange as it might seem, black or dark green vinyl coatings blend well with most landscapes (and

TYPICAL CHAIN LINK INSTALLATION

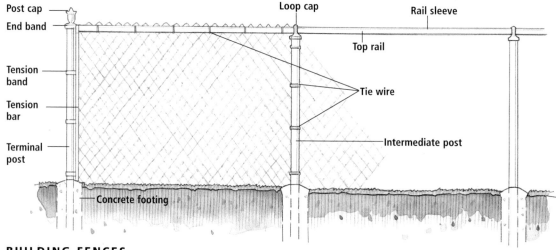

Post cap · End band · Tension band · Tension bar · Terminal post · Concrete footing · Loop cap · Top rail · Tie wire · Rail sleeve · Intermediate post

Plumb all posts with a level.

1 Lay out the fence line, spacing the postholes no more than 10 feet apart. Set the terminal (end) posts in concrete and let the concrete set. Then run a tight mason's line from the top of one terminal post to the other. Use this line to position, set, and plumb the intermediate posts at the correct height. Let the concrete cure for several days.

2 When the concrete has cured, slide tension bands down the terminal posts and fasten one end band loosely at the top of each terminal post. Cap these posts with post caps and place loop caps on the intermediate posts. Slide the top rail through the loop caps and into the end bands, joining the rail as necessary with rail sleeves. Level the rail and tighten the end bands securely.

actually may make the fence seem to disappear). You also have a choice in the size of the mesh opening—wider is cheaper, but smaller is more difficult to climb. A maximum opening of 1¼ inches is recommended for swimming pool fences unless you insert wood or plastic slats.

Wood-slat inserts, stained to resemble redwood, make chain link an attractive backdrop for vines. Plastic and metal inserts also come in a wide selection of colors. One variety makes the mesh look like a closely cropped hedge.

HOW TO USE
CHAIN LINK FENCE

■ **Defining spaces:** Good; but with a practical, not aesthetic, effect.

■ **Security:** Excellent for small children. Toddlers can learn to climb it, however.

■ **Privacy:** Poor; open infill provides very little privacy. Wood or vinyl inserts or plantings create privacy.

■ **Creating comfort zones:** Poor; open infill does not filter wind or sunlight.

3 Unroll the chain link mesh along the outside of the fence and lean it against the posts. Slide a tension bar through the end row of mesh.

Tension bar

Tension bands

Tension bar

4 Secure the bar inside the tension bands on one terminal post. Moving along the fence line, tie the mesh loosely to the top rail with tie wires.

5 Slide a stretching bar (or another tension bar) through the mesh about 3 or 4 feet from the next terminal post. Attach a fence stretcher or come-along (you can rent one) to the stretching bar and the terminal post. Tighten the mesh until you can squeeze an opening no more than about ½ inch. Unbend or cut the top and bottom links and unthread the surplus mesh. Slide a tension bar through the end and secure the tension bands to it. Tie the mesh to the top rail and posts.

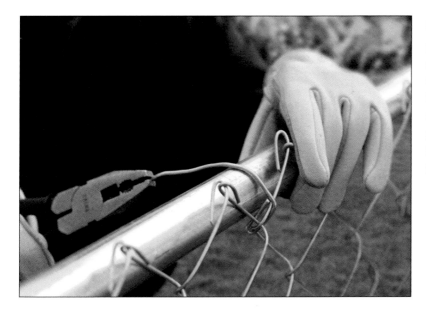

6 Tighten any rail ties previously installed and secure the top of the fence with additional ties, one every foot. To install the gate, first attach the fittings to the gate posts, then hang the gate on the hinges. Finally, set the gate latch.

DRESSING UP CHAIN LINK

You can improve the looks of your chain link fence and increase the privacy it offers by inserting wood or metal slats into the fabric. Cut the inserts to length and thread them through the mesh in a vertical or diagonal weave.

VIRGINIA ZIGZAG FENCES

Virginia zigzag fences (or worm fences) were a product of rural ingenuity, traditionally built from logs split in a triangular shape. The combination of the shapes of the rails and the angles of alternating courses kept the fence stable.

You can still buy 8- to 1-foot rails split from cedar or locust at some fencing outlets, but most rails today are of the sawn variety. Sawn rails don't have the same rustic appeal as their hand-hewn counterparts. Rails are moderately priced, but a fence requires a lot of lumber—total material costs can be high for a fence that runs a long distance. Pressure-treated landscape timbers are a less-expensive substitute. Construction is fairly time-consuming.

HOW TO USE
VIRGINIA ZIGZAG FENCES

- **Defining spaces:** Excellent; they make stunning rustic boundary markers.
- **Security:** Poor; they can impede access but are easy to climb over.
- **Privacy:** Poor; open rails provide no privacy.
- **Creating comfort zones:** Poor; open rails and low height do not filter wind or sunlight.

4x6 timber

10"

⁹⁄₁₆" or ¾" spade
bit on extender

1 Start by clamping (or holding) three 4×6 timbers with their edges and ends flush. Dill ⁹⁄₁₆-inch holes in both ends. You'll need a bit extender to drill through this thickness.

2 Distribute the rails along the fence line and drive one 5-foot length of rebar about 2 feet into the ground. Thread one end of a rail down on the rebar and position the rail on the fence line. Drive a second piece of rebar through the hole at the other end of the rail and into the ground. Reset the rail on both lengths of rebar, supporting it with blocks or rocks. Then slide one end of a second rail over the end of the first one, position it at about a 30-degree angle (or the angle of your choice), and support it with a 4×6 block. Drive rebar through the hole and into the ground.

3 Continue setting the rails on rebar until you have finished the first course. Then slide the rest of the rails over the rebar to complete the fence. Drive the rebar flush with the tops of the posts if necessary.

KENTUCKY RAIL FENCES

Kentucky rail (also called double-post-and-rail) fences represent an early form of post-and-rail construction. You can angle a Kentucky rail fence across your property, but its double-post design suits it to straight runs. Originally the bays were built to a length that suited whatever material was on hand. Today's versions are more modular: 8- to 12-foot bays are typical. Use split cedar (if you can afford it), treated round rails, or landscape timbers (4×6s are easy to handle). Set the posts so the rails will overlap one another by 12 to 18 inches. Rest the bottom rails on flat stones or fasten them to the posts. As an alternative to cinching the posts with wire, bridge them with wooden cleats.

HOW TO USE
KENTUCKY RAIL FENCES

■ **Defining spaces:** Excellent; they make stunning rustic boundary markers.

■ **Security:** Poor; they can impede access but are easy to climb over.

■ **Privacy:** Poor; open rails provide no privacy.

■ **Creating comfort zones:** Poor; open rails and low height do not filter wind or sunlight.

1 Lay out the fence line for 8- to 12-foot bays, locating the post holes so the posts will be set about a foot shorter than the length of the rails. Dig the holes and set the posts plumb in concrete or tamped earth and gravel. You can keep the posts properly spaced by inserting a 6× piece of rail or a post between them. Remove the spacer when the posts are braced and use it for the next pair.

2 Cut 4×6 timbers to length (if not using precut stock) and distribute them along the fence line. Set the bottom timbers on alternate bays, supporting them with rock or brick to keep them off the ground. Then set alternate courses between the posts until the fence is complete.

3 Wrap the top of each set of posts with #10 copper wire or soft iron wire and twist it tight with a lineman's pliers. Cut the posts at 36 inches (or about 4 inches higher than the top of the highest rail).

BAMBOO FENCES

Bamboo is a fast-growing tropical grass that displays amazing strength and weather resistance. These characteristics, along with the warm, soft golden color, make bamboo an excellent and unusual fencing material. Bamboo fences are stronger than wooden fences and if properly installed will outlast many wood species. Bamboo fencing comes in several forms: as rolled panels whose stakes are assembled with wire woven between them; as panels whose stakes are stapled to horizontal rails; and as panels woven with wire and framed by large poles on both ends. Panels are commonly 6 feet high and 6 or 8 feet long. How you install them depends on how the panel is constructed. You can even wire bamboo panels to a chain link fence with galvanized wire threaded through the mesh about every 4 or 5 inches at top, bottom, and middle. As with wooden infill, bamboo will deteriorate in direct contact with the ground—fasten the panels with their bottom edge 2 to 3 inches off the ground.

Some home centers and fencing supply outlets carry bamboo panels or can order them from a distributor. Mail-order fencing outlets are another good source. So is the Internet. Several manufacturers maintain websites, and you can order the fencing directly from them. All suppliers will provide you with design and construction details.

INSTALLING ROLLED BAMBOO

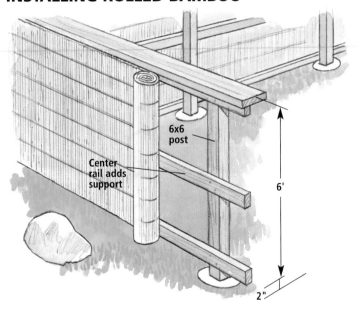

6x6 post

Center rail adds support

6'

2"

▲ Lay out the fence line for bays with interior dimensions equal to the width of the unrolled bamboo. Set the posts and build a flat-rail frame (page 134) with a center horizontal edge rail flush with the outside of the posts. Starting at one end of the fence, unroll the bamboo about a foot and tack it to the post. Unroll the panel to the other side and tack it. Then go back and fasten the panel to the rails, using the fastener recommended by the manufacturer and pulling the bamboo tight as you go.

▲ Bamboo fences and gates can add an oriental flair and privacy to a backyard landscape or water garden.

HOW TO USE
BAMBOO FENCES

- **Defining spaces:** Good; gives a pleasant, informal feeling of enclosure.
- **Security:** Fair; bamboo is extremely strong, but lower-quality fences can be easily disassembled by cutting the wires.
- **Privacy:** Excellent; bamboo provides a surface closed to outside views.
- **Creating comfort zones:** Good; can soften winds, block snow, and provide shade.

INSTALLING BAMBOO PANELS

Lay out the fence line with the post spacing specified by the manufacturer. Dig the holes and set the posts. Tack a level batten along the bottom of the posts and set the panel in place. Wire the panel to the posts and rails as shown. For panels with horizontal rails, predrill the ends of each rail and attach the rails to the posts with 2½-inch deck screws.

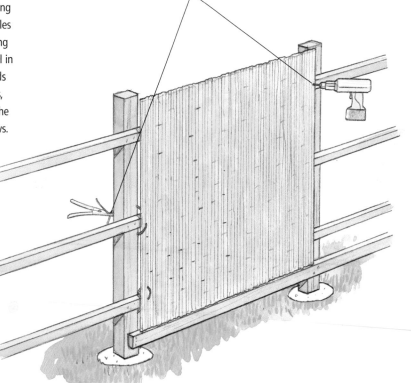

Attach the panels to the posts and rails with pieces of wire through the panel wire or drive 3" deck screws through the end frames

VARIATIONS ON YOUR FENCE THEME

Fences allow an almost infinite variety in their design. Each member of a fence structure—the posts, rails, and infill—can assume different shapes that will conform to your sense of style and fit the design parameters of your landscape plans.

Posts are a prime target for design alternatives. Milled post caps or finials will spice up your design with little effort. Finials (available at your home center) come in a wonderful array of configurations made to fit 4×4 or 6×6 posts. Most come complete with lag screws that hold the finial to the top of the post in a predrilled hole. Other styles rely on glued dowels to keep them in place. To keep rainwater from rotting the top of the post, caulk the bottom edge with silicone before tightening the finial. Post caps (also readily available) cover the top of the posts completely and shed rain from the end grain. You'll find them fluted, corniced, and chamfered (some with metal covers)—in

styles that match any fence design.

If you don't like what you see in the retail market, you can cut your own decorative shapes in the top of the posts. Chamfers are easily made by a table saw. So are any of a number of angled or beveled configurations and cornices. Rounded or globular shapes require a lathe. If you don't have the right equipment to decorate your own posts, you can probably find a local woodworker who will make them for a moderate fee.

Rail joints

How you join the rails to the posts can have a major impact on the appearance of your fence. Dadoes, through mortises, and channels (for panel or tongue-and-groove infill) will lend a touch of sophistication to your design. (They also will reduce maintenance costs because these joints are stronger than butt joints.)

POST CAP STYLES

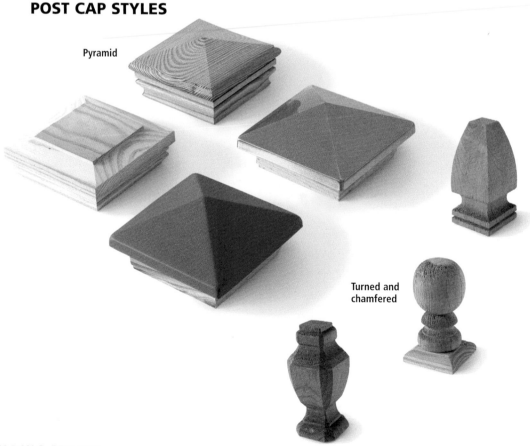

Pyramid

Turned and chamfered

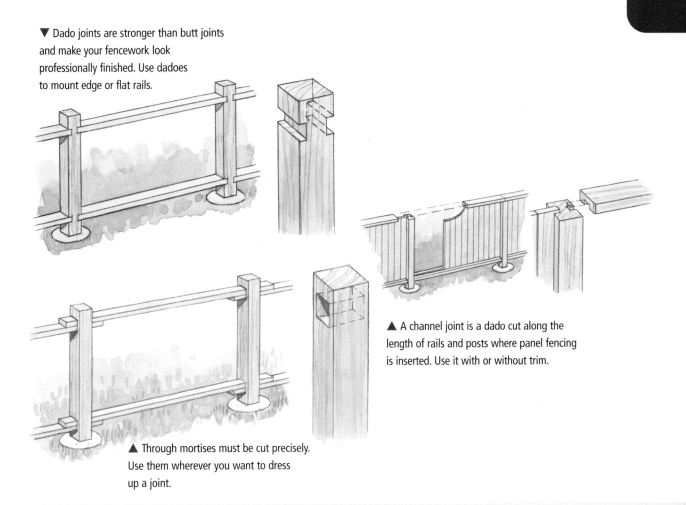

▼ Dado joints are stronger than butt joints and make your fencework look professionally finished. Use dadoes to mount edge or flat rails.

▲ A channel joint is a dado cut along the length of rails and posts where panel fencing is inserted. Use it with or without trim.

▲ Through mortises must be cut precisely. Use them wherever you want to dress up a joint.

AN EASY ALTERNATIVE

A woven lath fence is an inexpensive variation on the basic basket-weave design. It is also perhaps the easiest of all fences to construct. Aside from laying out the fence line and constructing a frame—which every fence requires—all you have to do is weave lath (1× stock ripped to ¼ or ³⁄₁₆ inch) between the rails. Friction does the rest—there's no need to fasten the rails. If they get knocked out of place from time to time, readjusting them takes only minutes. Because this design has so much visual texture, it will look best no more than 36 inches high. Posts can be square (4×4s) or round with mortised rails. Short bays (4 to 6 feet) will help break up the intricate visual rhythm of the weave.

WILD TOPS

Infill design

Infill is the most prominent feature of a fence and unfortunately is often the last one considered for variation. Scalloping the infill is a technique not necessarily limited to picket fences. It also can increase the visual interest of flush-mounted vertical infill. So can letting the tops run wild. You can install the boards at completely random heights over the entire length of the fence or design a regularly repeating pattern.

Leaving gaps between the boards on a fence or alternating boards with slats and leaving open spaces between them is another option. This technique gives the infill a sense of refinement and a pleasing visual rhythm, an ever-changing play of light and shadow.

Moreover it can make a long fence seem less imposing, and narrow spacing will help filter winds without compromising your privacy. It will also save you money because it takes less lumber than solid-board designs.

Either of these techniques (or both) will help solve problems when fencing a small area. Alternating the infill heights emphasizes the vertical dimension of the fence. Varying the width of the boards and leaving gaps between them reduces the tendency of the fence to look massive.

No matter how you end up adding variations to your fence—especially to the infill—you should experiment with your design on paper before purchasing your material. Grab your ¼-inch graph paper and draw the fence to scale. Make quick sketches of various ideas on tracing paper, then formalize your design to scale on the graph paper. There aren't any particular rules for this aspect of fence design. Style is often the result of creative choice.

SCALLOPED INFILL

OPEN TOPS

An unadorned board fence can appear massive and imposing, but you can soften that image by opening up the top of the fence. The look of a fence top will contribute as much to its overall style and appearance as the infill you select. Simplicity is the key throughout: Fence-top styles should provide a contrast, not a complication. Here are three ways to dress up your fence:

◀ **Blocked panel:** In this variation, 2×4 blocking at 3- to 4-foot intervals supports a 2×4 (or wider) cap rail. The blocks add an element of visual rhythm to the fence design and help keep the top rails from sagging.

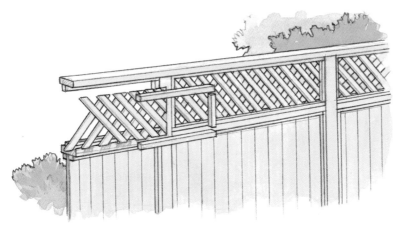

◀ **Lattice:** If you don't want a completely open top, install lattice. It affords some screening while it lets the light in and breaks up what otherwise might be an overwhelming stretch of tongue-and-groove or solid-board infill. After fastening a 2×6 top rail spanning the posts, install lattice panels in a frame of 1× stops (see page 48).

◀ **Arbor:** An arbor can bring an exciting contrast to any board fence. Make the supporting cleats from mitered 2×4s or 2×6s. The ends can be cut in decorative curves. Fasten the cleats to the post tops with carriage bolts. Predrill the 2×2 slats before attaching them to the cleats with screws.

CHAPTER HIGHLIGHTS

This chapter takes you through the

steps required for planning gates,

including aspects of style, materials,

and design. It also illustrates

step-by-step how to construct

any of several gate styles.

BUILDING GOOD GATES

Gates do more than just interrupt the line of a fence and provide a place of entry and exit. Whether it "disappears" into the fence line or stands out as an accent on its own, a gate is both a design and structural element that must integrate itself into the fence. Moreover, a gate must routinely endure loads and stresses that other parts of the fence are not subject to.

Even though it's usually the last element constructed in a fence project, a good gate cannot be an afterthought.

Gates call for thorough planning–right from the start–and careful construction–right to the end.

This chapter will help you plan the kind of gate you need–its location, size, direction of swing, and style. Then it will show you the techniques for building and installing various gate styles–sturdy, smooth-swinging structures whose designs you can use "as is" or modify to finish out your project perfectly.

DESIGNING A GATE

A gate is not an independent structure. It is an integral part of the overall fence system, and you should design it with that in mind. For such a small structure in a large expanse of lumber, planning a gate would seem to be an easy task. It's not.

Location

Your first consideration should be where to put the gate. This decision may already be made for you if the fence will cross an existing walkway. But if the walkway is not in place, you should plan the gate location and the path of the walkway in unison. Natural traffic patterns through the yard will provide a clue about the journey the path should take. Include any future plans you have for garden beds, decks, or patios.

Size

How large should your gate be? The answer depends on how you want to use the gate and what you want it to look like. To let two people pass comfortably, a gate needs a 4-foot opening. Gates that need to accommodate the passage of

▼ Gates can add style to what might otherwise be an average fence. This gate complements the picket fence; the arbor and flowering vine type add depth and color.

▲ Gates should be 4 feet wide for two people to pass through with ease or made wider to accommodate vehicles. This gate provides a grand entrance for visitors and is tall enough to provide security and privacy.

motorized garden or yard equipment might need to be as wide as 8 feet. In general, if your gate is wider than 4 feet, you'll need to support its end with a wheel, provide extra internal support, such as a turnbuckle, or span the opening with two panels. Keep in mind that as you go beyond 4 feet, you should start considering posts larger than 4×4s.

A front-yard gate—because of its prominence as the main entry to the house—may call for a more stylish design than a backyard gate leading to the garden shed. Here's where an ornamental metal gate on an ornamental metal fence makes an appropriate statement—inviting you in, but still defining the property boundaries with character. Unless privacy and security are your primary concerns, open fences with open gates are good choices for front yards. Backyard structures are commonly more closed because that's where most people want privacy and security.

Style

Style is an elusive quality, and in many cases achieving the style you want is simply an outgrowth of your instincts. There are, however, a few broad categories that can help you decide in a general way how you want your gate to look.

- **Contrast**–a gate designed as a contrast to the rest of the fence is a gate that calls attention to itself. You can create contrast by using a different material in the gate or using the same materials in a different way.
- **Complement**–a complementary gate employs the same material as the rest of the fence and is designed to look like a fence bay. A complementary style is often a necessity and coincides with the purpose of a security fence.
- **Combination**–a gate that blends in with the general appearance of the fence but uses a special element (such as a lattice top panel) becomes an interesting element in its own right without competing with the fence.

◀ Ideally a walkway and a gate are planned simultaneously; landscaping plans should be considered during the design phase too. This gate contrasts with the brick columns, the curved walkway, and the garden it protects.

THE STRUCTURE OF A GATE

Gates, like a fence bay, are an individual structural system composed of framing, infill, and bracing (when necessary). Gates place a heavy load on their fences, and gate posts are often larger and set deeper than terminal or intermediate posts.

The hardware you use to hinge and latch the gate possesses an aesthetic quality all its own, but when you choose hardware make sure it's sized appropriately to your gate in addition to matching its style.

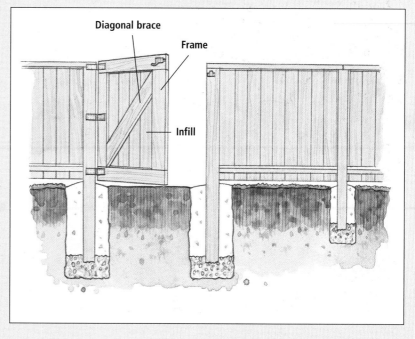

Diagonal brace

Frame

Infill

DESIGNING A GATE (CONTINUED)

Swing

Which way the gate should swing will depend on where it's located. In some locations, like a front-yard entry, a gate with an inappropriate swing can just be an inconvenience. In other locations, a gate that swings the "wrong" way can pose a safety hazard and invite serious injury. Most outdoor gates will swing only one way. If you need a gate that swings both ways, you can purchase spring-loaded hinges that return the gate to its "neutral" position after opening it (see "Self-closing Hinges," page 93).

DOWN A SLOPE

▲ Gates that follow a fence line down a slope can open or close as their purpose dictates. For example, a sloped property-line gate should probably swing inward. What's more important is that you hinge a sloped gate on the downhill side. That way the bottom of the fence won't get caught on the slope when you open it. Build the frame square, not contoured, so the gate will get the support it needs to keep it from sagging. A gate on a slope is essentially a perimeter-framed gate with infill fastened to correspond to the plane of the slope.

BOUNDARY-LINE FENCES

▲ Gates installed in a property-line fence are usually mounted so they swing into the property. Fences that separate areas within a property, such as those between the "entertainment" and "service" areas of a yard, might experience high traffic. Here's where a gate that swings both ways can greatly increase convenience. For example, it's a lot easier to bump through a double-action gate with an armload of groceries than it is to grasp for a latch. Incorporate a see-through opening in the design of a double-swinging gate so that people on both sides can see when someone is coming through.

WHERE FENCES MEET

◄ A gate placed near the corner of a perpendicular intersection of fence lines should swing to the corner so it's out of the way when open.

TOP OR BOTTOM OF STAIRS

▲ If the landing is wider than the swing of the gate, you can safely mount a gate at the top or bottom of a stairway. What matters is that the landing is wide enough to provide a "signal" that stairs follow it, either up or down.

PERPENDICULAR TO A SLOPE

◄ Gates hung perpendicular to a slope must swing to the downhill side. They won't open all the way if they swing uphill.

AN ALPHABET OF GATE FRAMES—BEGINNING WITH Z

Because of the arrangement of their parts, the construction of gate frames resembles letters in the alphabet. Z-frame gates are the most common, followed by X- and H-frames. Although they may look the same, there are some definite differences.

■ Z-frames are easiest to build; they have the fewest parts.

■ Z-frame gates are not as strong as X- and H-frames.

■ A Z-frame looks light and casual. X- and H-frames can look stocky.

■ All these frames can handle surface-mounted infill, but only an H-frame will accept inset infill.

HARDWARE AND LATCHES

G ate hardware is as much a design element as any other part of the fence or gate structure. Hinges and latches are the icing on the cake. They give the gate design a detail or accent that embellishes the appearance of the entire structure. But with gate hardware, even the most delicate ornaments have a hefty job to do. When you're shopping for hardware, make your choices based on appearance and ruggedness.

So many kinds of hinges and latches exist that they defy categorization. Many latches are designed for operation from one side only. For example, a simple hook-and-eye latch, a slide-action latch, and a striker all operate conveniently from only one side. To open them from the "wrong" side of the fence, you have to reach over the top of the gate. A top latch will solve this problem. So will a lever-action latch.

Specialty hardware or restoration catalogs are good places to look for attractive or unusual hardware. Ornamental iron shops—or even a brass foundry—will make just about anything you want. You'll pay more, of course, but the cost might be worth it for that one-of-a-kind design. Don't forget antique shops, salvage yards, and building-material recycling centers.

Latches

Like most aspects of fence planning, it's usually not wise to buy a latch without first considering how easy it is to operate, how securely it closes, and how it fits the style of the gate.

In some cases the gate size will affect your choice of latches. If the gate is tall, for example, and you can't reach over it to get at the latch, you need one that can be operated from both sides.

For security, some latches include locks or hasps for a padlock. Make sure you can unlock the gate from the inside so getting in or out is easy in an emergency. Check local codes for requirements that apply to gate exit and entry.

Hinges

Even though you can construct a gate from a variety of different materials, there's no such thing as a "light" gate. By its very nature, a gate is subject to stresses from more factors than its weight, and the first place a gate will try to relieve its stress is on the hinges. Three hinges hang a gate far better than two. Err on the side of excess when you select the hinges and fasteners–make "heavy-duty" and "heavy gauge" part of your selection criteria.

Fasteners

Most latches and hinges will come with their own fasteners, and most fasteners are woefully undersized. The screws may fit the holes, but they are not nearly long enough to hold the hinge securely. Screws should penetrate the wood frame as deeply as possible without going through the other side.

If the screws supplied with your hinges or latch aren't long enough to do the job, buy replacements of the same gauge, but longer. Using the same gauge will ensure that the screw fits snugly in the mounting hole and, in the case of hinges, sets flush with the hinge plate. Finding replacements for fasteners made to match the style of decorative hinges may be difficult. Sometimes an exact match isn't necessary. In this instance just get the closest match you can.

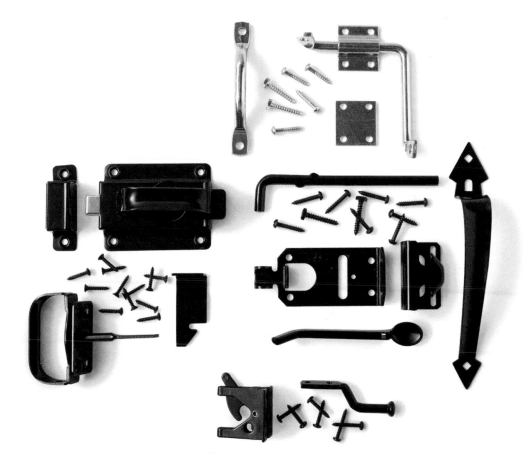

BUILDING A BRACED-FRAME GATE

A lmost all gates will need some form of diagonal bracing–which is always installed with the lower end of the diagonal on the hinge side. The style of gate illustrated above employs double diagonals, although in truth, the second diagonal adds more to the aesthetics of the gate than to the strength.

The benefit of a braced-frame gate is that it can accept any kind of infill and therefore can be used with any style fence. It's also rugged enough to support the weight of infill up to a size of 3 feet by 6 feet.

Measure the gate opening before you cut the framing. Take measurements between the posts at both the top and bottom. If the measurements are different, it means one or both of the posts are not plumb. Hanging a gate on tilted posts will make the gate look as though it's sagging (and, in fact, it will eventually sag). You can make a slight adjustment by shimming out the hinges to level the gate, but you should replace or straighten a post that's severely out of plumb (see page 160). Once you have the measurements straight, subtract the amount of clearance and use this dimension to cut the framing.

Be sure to use kiln-dried lumber for the frame and cut the rails the full width of the frame. Cut the stiles to a length that will put the gate rails on the same plane as the fence rails. You can use butt joints as shown below, miter the corners for a cleaner look, or half-lap them for added strength. To make your gate even stronger, apply polyurethane glue to the joints before fastening them.

Because lumber is not a perfect medium, sometimes the infill boards will not fit flush with the sides of the gate in the prescribed number, no matter how carefully you measured and calculated. In every case it's best to cut the infill to length and dry-lay it on the frame. If it's a little too wide you can rip each board or space them a little differently.

1 Measure the gate opening with clearances and cut the frame to fit, with butted or mitered corners. Square the frame and fasten the corners with two predrilled screws.

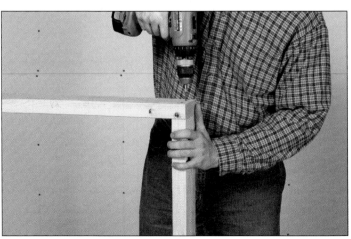

Crosspiece
centered
under corner
of frame

2 Support the frame on 2× blocks and center the 2×4 crosspiece under opposite corners. Make sure the frame is still square, then mark the angles at the ends of the crosspiece.

3 Test-fit the crosspiece in the corners. It should slide in snugly, but without contorting the frame.

4 Using the same techniques as you did in Step 1, mark and cut the other diagonal. Cut a half lap in the center of one piece and use it to mark the other. Then cut a half lap in this diagonal too. The half-lapped joint will allow the brace to fit flush in the frame.

5 Fasten the brace to the frame by driving predrilled screws through the corners into the ends of the brace. Then cinch the half-lap joint with a predrilled 2½-inch screw.

6 Cut the gate infill boards to the length required by your design. Fasten them to the frame and brace with predrilled 3-inch screws.

BUILDING A Z-FRAME GATE

A Z-frame gate is a braced-frame gate without the sides. Because it uses a little less lumber, it's a little less expensive (and a little less strong) than a braced-frame gate. It brings a distinctive style to a gate, one reminiscent of the doors on farm structures.

Use kiln-dried lumber for the gate and lay out the infill to match the dimensions of the gate opening—less the clearances required on either side (page 92). If the width of the infill exceeds the final dimensions of the gate, you can rip the difference equally from the end boards. That way the infill will look balanced.

When you set the rails in place, position them so they're on the same plane as the fence rails. At this stage you can increase the strength of the gate by running a bead of construction adhesive across the infill at the center of the rail location. When the adhesive cures, it won't "give" as much as the fasteners will under the stresses of the gate. Apply the adhesive to the diagonals too.

1 Measure the gate opening with the proper clearances, then lay out the infill boards, spacing them to fit the dimensions of the opening. Square the boards with a framing square and clamp them together with a pipe clamp.

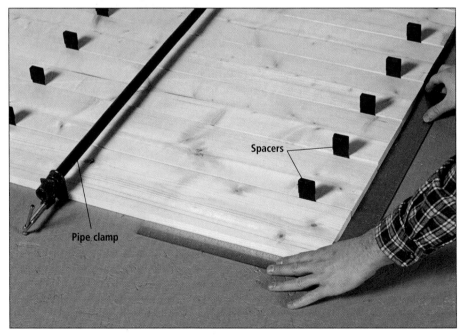

Spacers

Pipe clamp

2 Cut the top and bottom 2×4 rails to fit the dimensions of the infill (or slightly smaller if required by your design). Position the rails on the infill and tack them at each board. Remove the spacers.

Bottom rail

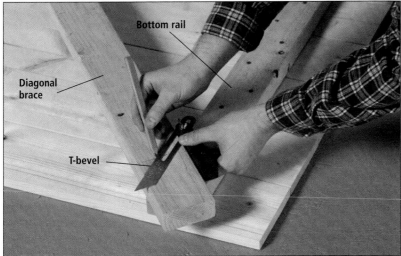

Bottom rail

Diagonal brace

T-bevel

3 Keeping the gate square, set the diagonal brace on the infill (with the bottom of the brace on the hinge side and the top on the latch side). Mark the angle for its cut. Using a T-bevel will ensure that both angles are identical.

4 Tack the diagonal brace to the infill between the top and bottom rails. Then secure the joints by driving angled screws into the ends of the diagonal. Flip the gate over and secure the infill to the frame with two screws at each board.

BUILDING A DIAGONAL SOLID-CORE GATE

A diagonal solid-core gate needs no external bracing. The diagonal orientation of the infill boards supplies the necessary bracing against the stresses of the gate.

You can build this gate with 1×4 or 1×6 boards (the scale of 1×4s will likely look more appealing), or tongue-and-groove boards. Tongue-and-groove stock will increase the strength of the gate—the friction between the mating surfaces will add to its stability. Make the gate even stronger by applying polyurethane glue to the tongues as you fasten the infill.

Because this design is inherently stronger than framed gates, it will span wider openings (which may require 6×6 posts), and the design is a good candidate for a double gate. Installing the gates with the diagonals running in opposite directions will increase the interest of the installation.

When you measure the gate opening, subtract the necessary clearances (page 92) and an additional 1½ inches to allow for the thickness of the trim. Be sure to install the gate with the diagonals running down toward the hinge side.

1 Measure the gate opening and, allowing the proper clearances, cut the frame members to these dimensions. Lay out the frame on a flat surface and square the corners with a framing square.

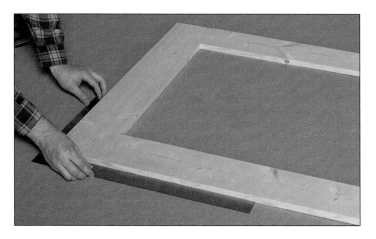

Corner brace

2 Keeping the corners square, cut corner braces and secure them to the frame on diagonal corners. Set the first piece of infill against the edge of one corner piece and mark the angle at which you will cut both ends. Cut the board at both ends and fasten it to the frame. Continue installing the infill until you have filled the frame.

Side trim

3 Cut a piece of side trim equal to the height of the frame. Fasten it with predrilled screws driven through the infill and into the bottom frame members. Measure, cut, and install the remaining trim.

1x edge trim

4 Trim 1× stock to the width of the frame and cut the edge trim for all four sides to the dimensions of the gate. Fasten the edge trim to the frame with predrilled screws.

BUILDING A PANELED GATE

A paneled gate starts out as a framed gate, but incorporates one or more rails between the top and bottom rail, dividing the gate into sections.

Because this style puts the infill in the center of a flat-rail frame, it adds visual interest to the gate. Even if the infill materials are the same as used in the fence bays, it will look different because it's not on the same plane as the fence. A lattice-and-board combination will lighten the visual appearance of the gate while preserving the feeling of security.

You can use any material in any of the panels, but if you use lattice in the largest panel, you may want to add diagonal bracing. Vertical boards or tongue-and-groove infill will increase the strength of the gate, because the surface of the infill works against the frame. Diagonal boards will provide the most strength.

The key to this construction is using 1× stops to contain the infill. In effect, the infill is sandwiched between the stops, although you don't want to nail the infill to the stops–they will split. Toenail the infill to the frame.

To locate the stops, subtract the total thickness of the infill and the stops from the width of the frame (3½ inches). Divide the result by 2 to compute the "reveal"–the amount of space between the edge of the frame and the edge of the stop. The reveal itself becomes an additional stylistic element because it adds another line and dimension to the design. You can butt-joint the stops in the corners, but your gate will look better if you miter the stops. Arranging spacers around the frame as shown will make the installation of the stops more accurate. If you don't have spacer stock the same thickness as the reveal, you can rip some from scrap 1×4s.

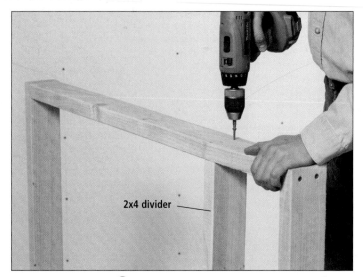

1 Measure the gate opening and cut 2×4 frame members to fit, allowing for the proper clearances. Fasten the outer frame members with butted, mitered, or half-lapped corners. Square the frame with a framing square, then measure, cut, and install the 2×4 divider 10 to 12 inches below the top of the frame.

2x4 divider

1x stop

Spacer

2 Measure and miter 1× stops to fit the internal openings of the frame. Set spacers equal to the reveal around the frame. Setting the stops on the spacers, fasten all the stops with finishing nails. If you predrill the stops and insert all the finishing nails into them, nailing the stops will be easier.

3 Cut the lattice panel to fit using a circular saw and lay it in the upper frame opening. Secure the panel with stops on this side. Cut and install the lower panel infill, sandwiching it between stops as you did in the upper opening.

TIPS FOR A TIP-TOP GATE

Each kind of gate construction uses slightly different techniques. Here are some tips that apply to all gates:

■ Make sure your frame stock will support its load. You'll find very few gates with frames thinner than 2×4s. But even 2×4s might be too small on a large gate with heavy infill.

■ Buy the best wood you can afford. Heartwood of redwood or cedar, or pressure-treated lumber, is less likely to warp or rot.

■ Make sure all your hardware is rust and corrosion resistant—maintaining and repairing inexpensive hardware will cost you in the long run.

■ Do you want to latch your gate open (in addition to being able to latch it closed)? A hook-and-eye will do the trick. So will a J-latch or cane bolt. They slip into a pipe in the ground.

■ For automatic gate-closing, use a gate spring—one that's strong enough to push the latch closed.

■ To minimize sag on a long gate that swings over a smooth surface, put a wheel near the end of the gate.

HANGING A GATE

anging a gate proceeds in a fairly straightforward manner. To begin the process, you'll have to jockey the gate into position. Start by supporting the gate within the opening. Set 2×4s under each end of the bottom rail (supporting an overhanging infill will only tip the gate one way or the other). Add 2×4s until you get the bottom rail within ¼ inch of level with the bottom rail of the fence. Then work tapered shims on top of both sides of the 2×4s (if possible) until the rail is in place. Shim the sides.

Start with a thin, straight piece of 1× stock and insert tapered shims until both sides of the gate are set at the correct clearances (see page 92). Even though the gate may seem solidly wedged in the opening, have a helper hold it while you predrill the hardware holes and tighten the screws.

Most butt hinges will support the gate properly if you install them 4 to 6 inches from the top and bottom of the gate. T-hinges and strap hinges are made so their "straps" are mounted on the rails. Whatever kind of hinge you use, fasten it to the post first, then the gate.

Swing the gate open and closed to make sure it moves smoothly, doesn't bind, and clears the opening evenly. If it doesn't, adjust the position of the hinge or insert shims under the plates. When you're satisfied that the gate swings properly, install the latch.

If you have designed your gate so that it stops on 2× stock and you haven't fastened the stop, do so now.

Cut the stop 1 inch longer than the height of the gate and mark its position on the gate post. Hold the stop on the line and predrill the first hole through the stop and the post about 1 inch from the top of the stop. Fasten the stop to the post with predrilled 3½-inch screws driven every 6 inches. On a wide surface, such as a masonry wall, use a 2×4 for the top and mount it with countersunk lag screws.

JOINTS AND CLOSURES

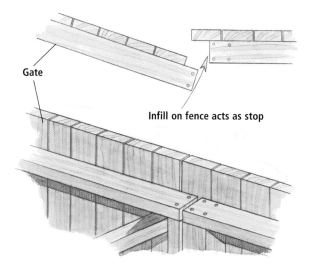

Gate

Infill on fence acts as stop

▲ In this style the gate swings to the outside of the fence, and when it closes, the extended edge of the fence infill acts as a stop. This method will work with both edge- and flat-rail gate frames.

▼ In this style, for a flat-rail gate frame, the gate closes toward the inside of the fence, and the edge of an infill board acts as a stop.

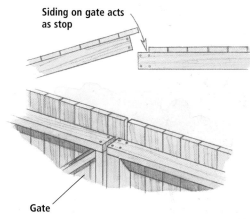

Siding on gate acts as stop

Gate

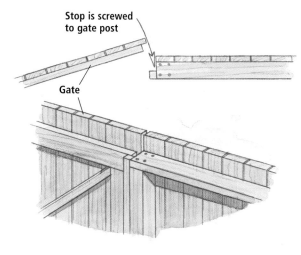

Stop is screwed to gate post

Gate

▲ This the gate closes from the outside of the fence and is stopped by 2x stock screwed to the fence post. This method is limited to edge-rail gate frames.

▼ If your gate swings to the outside of the fence, you can stop it with a board fastened to the inside face of the post. This method can be used with a flat-rail gate frame only if the gate is set back from the front of the fence.

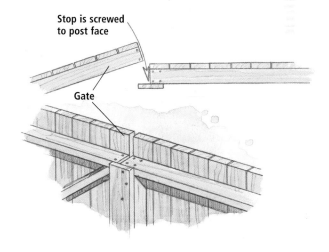

Stop is screwed to post face

Gate

1 Hanging a gate can easily be a one-person job if you insert shims and blocks to support the gate. Using shims to keep the gate spaced properly is a good idea, even if you have help. The shims assure you a proper fit. Measure, mark, and install the hinges, predrilling the holes for fasteners.

½" to ⅝" clearance on the latch side

¼" to ½" clearance on the hinge side

Latch

Hold strike in open position and drill hole in post for cord. Run cord through the post and tie it to the "eye" of the strike. Pull cord to open the gate from the outside.

Strike bar

2 Mark the location of the latch on the inside of the gate (the gate shown above opens out). Drill holes for the mounting screws and fasten the latch.

3 Hold the strike bar on the post and close the gate so the latch engages. Position the strike bar to allow free movement of the latch when opening and closing. Mark the mounting holes on the post, predrill them, and fasten the strike bar with screws.

HANGING A GATE ON MASONRY

1 Drill centered holes (counterbored if desired) in a 2×6 cleat and use these holes to drill locator holes on the masonry surface. Holding the cleat plumb, drill the locator holes with a hammer drill and masonry bit. Remove the cleat and drill holes in the masonry deep enough to accept the anchors. Insert the anchors in the holes and tap them flush with a hammer.

2 Position the cleat with the holes lined up, insert a lag screw with washer into the anchors, and tighten the lag screw with a socket wrench. Install the remaining lag screws in the same manner.

SELF-CLOSING HINGES

Self-closing hinges can greatly increase the convenience of a gate. They can't be used on gates whose location permits only a one-way swing, but they can make getting the groceries through the garage gate and into the house easier. Coupled with a self-closing latch, they'll keep the gate closed in windy climates, and that will make your gate last a lot longer.

Choose between the spring-loaded barrel hinge and an external spring. The performance of both is roughly the same, so base your choice on how well the device works with the style of your gate and hardware.

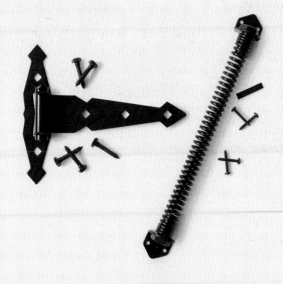

CHAPTER HIGHLIGHTS

This chapter takes you through all the basics associated with building fences—from choosing the right lumber to laying out the site and assembling the fence. Whether you're new to outdoor construction or an old hand at it, you'll find more than a tip or two that will make the job easier.

BUILDING BASICS

A well-built, handsome fence is the product of careful planning and attention to details. It requires craftsmanship and skill. If you're new to construction or just a little rusty, this chapter can help develop those skills. It contains all the information you need to learn how to use the hand tools and power tools required for building a fence.

Nothing, however, develops skills more quickly than practice. So start slowly and take your time until you feel proficient. Minimize distractions and nonproductive activity by keeping the work site organized. Always put each tool back in the same place when you're done with it. That way you won't waste time trying to find the tool when you need it. Strap on a comfortable tool belt and keep basic tools–tape measure, pencil, knife, layout square, and hammer–in assigned pockets. Jot down measurements rather than trying to memorize them. That will allow you to think about important things rather than trying to remember a number.

Master these building basics and you'll be able to construct any of the fences featured in this book and just about any outdoor structure you can dream up.

LANDSCAPING TOOLS

The list of landscaping tools is a short one, but each of the tools shown below is indispensible in constructing a fence. Make sure their cutting edges are sharp–tools that cut cleanly through soil and sod will save a great deal of time and effort.

Drain spade. With its narrow, pointed blade, a drain spade is ideal for breaking sod and starting postholes. It also comes in handy in other tight spots, such as shoveling soil or concrete around posts that you're setting.

Hand auger. This one is designed to bore holes in the soil with repeated turns of the handle. Set the point in the soil, give it a turn, lift it out of the hole, knock dirt from the blades, and repeat the process until you've reached the depth you want. You can make the job easier by renting a power auger (opposite).

Clamshell posthole digger. A pair of long-handled shovels hinged together offers an efficient way to dig postholes. You open the shovel blades, drive them into the ground, push the handles apart, and lift out a chunk of earth. (You may need to rotate the blades back and forth to cut roots or dislodge small rocks.)

Round-nosed shovel. Use this workhorse for all sorts of digging jobs. A long-handled version provides increased leverage. A square-blade spade (not shown) is best for cutting through sod roots if you're removing a large area.

Drain spade

Hand auger

Clamshell posthole digger

Iron rake

Round-nosed shovel

Tamper

Trowel

Iron rake. Also known as a bow rake or garden rake, an iron rake breaks up and levels soil.

Tamper. Compact soil around posts and in other spots that require firm, dense earth. You can make your own tamper by screwing two 10-inch squares of ¾-inch plywood to one end of a 2×4.

Trowel. Move small amounts of soil in tight spots with this basic gardener's tool. It also comes in handy for cleaning up the sides of postholes and for mixing concrete and placing it around posts.

Buying tips

Examine tools before you buy. Make sure the tool fits you–if a handle is too long or short, try another. Check the quality of the connection between the handle and "business end" of the tools. Avoid inexpensive handles–you'll soon end up back at your home center for a more durable model. Look for handles that are stamped "hickory."

Remember that most manufacturers offer several lines of tools at various price levels. It's not a bad idea to buy an inexpensive version of a tool you'll use only a few times, but spend more on high-quality tools you'll use often.

Caring for landscaping tools

Well-made tools last for years if you don't abuse or neglect them. Here are some maintenance hints:
■ Clean tools after each use with a paint stick or steel brush to keep soil from encrusting.
■ Wipe wooden handles with linseed oil, then wipe off the excess oil. Paint tools a bright color if you tend to lose them.
■ Sharpen tools for efficiency and safety. Usually you can do the job with a metal file.
■ Check and tighten bolts and screws regularly.
■ For safety and to maintain cutting edges, hang tools on the wall of your garage or shed. Protect steel blades against rust by applying a light coat of machine oil.

POWER POSTHOLE DIGGERS

If you have several postholes to dig, consider renting one of these gasoline-powered machines. Power augers come with interchangeable spiral boring bits for making holes 6, 8, or 10 inches in diameter. They can excavate holes up to 44 inches deep. Some models, like the one above right, can be operated by one person. The larger auger, above left, takes two people to operate but is less likely to kick out of a hole when it hits a rock or tree root.

To dig with a power auger, mark the depth of the posthole on the bit with tape and center the tip of the auger on the posthole location. Start the engine, adjust the speed with the handle-mounted throttle, and exert even downward pressure. After digging a few inches, slowly raise the bit to dislodge dirt from the hole.

Layout and Measuring Tools

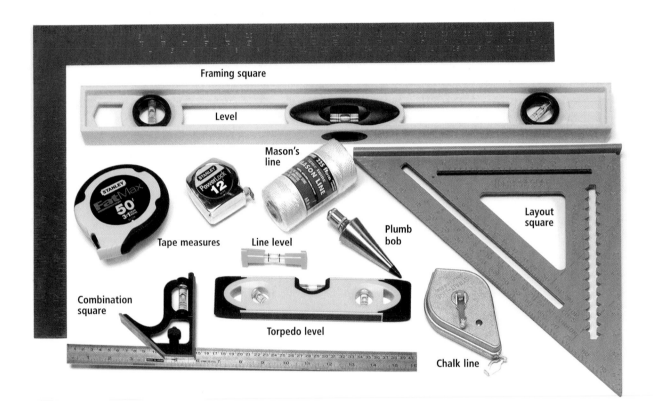

Framing square

Level

Mason's line

Tape measures

Line level

Plumb bob

Layout square

Combination square

Torpedo level

Chalk line

The tools shown above represent the basic kit for fencing projects. You may already have many of them in your toolbox, but if you don't, buy the best tools you can afford. A tool that won't stand up to the rigors of your project will cost you time and money—and most often will fail right in the middle of an important phase of your project.

During the course of your project, you may end up relying on more than one tool to take measurements. Before you start, line up all the measuring tools you might use and make sure their scales are the same. You may be surprised to find that different rulers can vary as much as ⅛ inch from one to the other. If they are not the same, remove all but one from the work site.

Framing square. Also called a carpenter's square, a framing square is designed for squaring almost anything. Its size makes it ideal for squaring large corners and marking sheet material, such as plywood. Framing squares are also stamped with rulers that you can use to measure.

Level. Levels come in various lengths, and you may need more than one, depending on the nature of your project. A short **torpedo level** can fit where a longer level can't. The longest model, a 4-foot carpenter's level, provides accuracy over broad spans. Use the vials on either end of the level to check for plumb; the center vial is for checking level. Some models are equipped with 45-degree vials as well.

Tape measure. If you're laying out a long fence line, a 50-foot or longer cloth or flexible steel tape with a locking device saves time. For measuring the distance between posts and the length of lumber, use a 12- or 25-foot tape. A locking feature holds the tape in position while you make your mark.

Mason's line. A woven line made specifically for layout, mason's line is strong, has limited "stretch," and won't sag when tied tightly. Laying out a fence line is next to impossible without it. Coupled with the **line level** shown below it, opposite, a mason's line lets you determine level over a long distance, such as between post tops. The level clips onto the line.

Plumb bob. For determining or marking a perfectly vertical line (or to mark post locations), use a plumb bob suspended on a length of mason's line.

Layout square. This tool features a flange or "heel" along one edge that keeps it butted up against the edge of a board when marking angles. You can also use it as a guide to keep cuts straight when you're using a circular saw.

Chalk line. Use this for marking long, straight lines on large materials such as plywood or for marking the height of posts. Hook the end over an edge, stretch the line tight against the surface, lift, and snap it to mark the line.

Combination square. Square and mark boards for crosscuts with a combination square. It also may be used as a marking and depth gauge and for laying out 45-degree miters. Most combination squares include a level in the handle, but this has limited use in fence building.

LASER LEVELS

Traditional bubble levels are precision instruments, but they have one notable limitation—their length. The longest of them, a carpenter's level, is 4 feet long. That means when you need to draw a long level line—on the side of a building, for example—you have to slide the level along the surface. Every time you move it, you risk an inaccuracy that will compound as you progress. Laser levels project a colored light beam on a surface that's as long or high as the surface itself. Some models employ a buzzer that sounds when the line is level or plumb—a handy feature if you're working in low light or in an awkward position.

CARPENTRY HAND TOOLS

Although it's true that the variety of power tools in today's market has made many jobs easier and faster, power tools still haven't put hand tools out of business. That's because there are some jobs that power tools can't do or can't do well–clamping, for instance, or driving stakes. For other tasks, such as sawing a single board, cutting with a handsaw is actually faster than getting out your circular saw and setting it up. Here are descriptions of the hand tools shown:

Jack plane. Measuring 12 to 15 inches long, a jack plane makes a good general-use smoothing tool. A block plane, with its low blade angle, is good for end-grain planing.

Crosscut saw. A crosscut saw is designed specifically for cutting across the grain, the most common cutting operation.

Ripsaw. You can use a crosscut saw to rip a board–saw with the grain–but you'll make slow headway. A ripsaw cuts best with the grain.

Toolbox saw. This stubby model, so called because it will fit into a tool box (albeit a large one) is a hybrid saw designed for both crosscutting and rip cutting. If there's only one saw you can afford, get this one.

Miter box and backsaw. Use these to make square and angled cuts in narrow lumber, such as trim or tenons. The box guides the cuts; the saw–a small crosscut saw with a reinforced back that keeps it from bending–does the work.

Sanding block. Sandpaper works best when it's held flat against the surface. Buy a wood, plastic, or rubber sanding block or wrap sandpaper around a block of wood.

3-pound sledge. Sometimes called a baby sledge, this hefty hammer easily handles heavy-duty pounding jobs, such as driving stakes.

Curved-claw hammer. Make a 16-ounce curved-claw hammer your first tool purchase. Besides driving nails, a claw hammer also pulls them.

Ripping-claw hammer. Use a 20-ounce hammer with a ripping claw for driving framing nails and prying boards apart.

Nail set. Countersink or set nails beneath the wood's surface with this inexpensive tool.

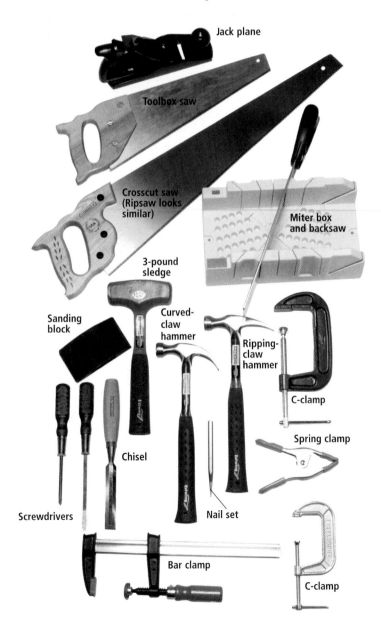

Jack plane

Toolbox saw

Crosscut saw
(Ripsaw looks
similar)

Miter box
and backsaw

3-pound
sledge

Sanding
block

Curved-
claw
hammer

Ripping-
claw
hammer

C-clamp

Spring clamp

Chisel

Nail set

Screwdrivers

Bar clamp

C-clamp

Screwdrivers. You'll need straight and phillips heads for attaching hardware.

Chisels. Use a chisel when you need to cut mortises for hinges, remove excess wood from grooves and joints, shape joints, form inside and outside curves in wood, or trim wood to close tolerances. Chisels with ¼- ⅜-, ½-, and ¾-inch-wide blades, often sold in sets, will perform most chiseling chores.

Clamps. An assortment of clamps is essential for holding materials together or supporting them while you drill, saw, screw, or nail them. C-clamps, spring clamps, and bar clamps are handy types to have.

Buying tips

Take your time when purchasing any tool–you'll encounter several different alloys.
■ **Carbon steel** is fine for screwdrivers and other tools that don't generate heat and for tools that will not see frequent use. It is generally not a cost-effective purchase.
■ **Low-alloy steel** includes some tungsten or molybendum to increase durability.
■ **High-alloy steel**, which has a much higher tungsten or molybendum content, is the best choice for high-speed cutting tools. Power saw blades tipped with tungsten carbide will last the average do-it-yourselfer for years.

Metal tools differ, too, in the way they're made. Casting, the least expensive manufacturing technique, can result in flaws in the metal that make it liable to chip and break. If you'll be hitting or applying muscle to the tool, don't buy the cast type. A broken tool can cause serious injury.

Forged or drop-forged tools are almost indestructible. Chisels should be made of high-quality steel with precisely ground bevels and edges.

Don't overlook a tool made partly of plastic either. For instance, fiberglass handles on

JAPANESE PULL SAWS

These thin-blade saws cut on the pull stroke, not the push stroke like traditional Western saws. This prevents the blade from buckling and binding, providing more control. The saw can't jump out of its groove and cause damage to the project or the user's hands.

■ The unusual blade design works equally well for both crosscutting and rip cutting, undercuts, and reverse cuts. Some Japanese saw blades have a single cutting edge; others have teeth for ripping on one side, crosscutting on the other. Others are made with a flexible blade that will bend sufficiently to allow you to cut dowels flush with the surrounding surface.
■ It's difficult to sharpen these fine-tooth saws, so most have replaceable blades.

hammers are every bit as strong as steel shanks, yet they have even more resilience than old-fashioned wood handles and deliver less shock to your hand and arm.

POWER TOOLS

For most jobs, power tools allow you to get the work done faster and easier—and frequently more accurately. Most of the power tools you'll need will be portable, making them easy to store and carry to the job site. A few fencing tasks will also go more smoothly with a table saw and power miter saw. If you don't have them and don't want to make the investment, consider renting or borrowing them for the short time they're needed.

Drill/driver. A cordless drill/driver is the most versatile tool you can have in your tool kit. Drills for home use come with $\frac{1}{4}$-, $\frac{3}{8}$-, and $\frac{1}{2}$-inch chuck capacity and an adjustable clutch you can set to release when the screw head is flush with the wood. You can handle most fence-building tasks with a $\frac{3}{8}$-inch chuck, but if you're buying a new drill, you may find that

some manufacturers are phasing out $\frac{3}{8}$-inch models in favor of the more powerful and more useful 18-volt $\frac{1}{2}$-inch variety. Whatever you buy, get one with a spare battery.

Drill bits. You'll need a variety of small and medium-size twist bits to predrill holes for nails and screws. You'll also need spade bits if you plan to counterbore any machine screw heads or lag screws. If your fence will be attached to brick or other masonry, you'll need masonry bits. And of course you'll need phillips and/or square-drive screwdriver bits to drive screws.

Circular saw. For most chores use a $7\frac{1}{4}$-inch model with a carbide-tipped combination blade. If you're in the market for a new saw, make sure the blade guard retracts smoothly and the bevel and saw-plate clamps lock easily but

Router

$7\frac{1}{4}$" circular saw

Belt sander

Spade bits

Masonry bit

Screwdriver bits

Twist drill

Cordless drill/driver

Jigsaw

securely. Most of all buy a saw with a good feel to it.

Jigsaw. A lightweight jigsaw can crosscut, rip, miter, bevel, and cut curves in almost any material. Only one hand is needed to guide a jigsaw. Most cuts can be made quickly and accurately, especially if you have a rip-guide accessory.

Sanders. For smoothing large areas (refinishing an old gate panel, for example), you might need a **belt sander**, but be careful because this tool does such an efficient job of removing material, your biggest problem may be controlling it. A light-duty finishing sander or orbital sander is a better choice for most projects. Whatever sander you use, make sure it has a dust bag. The bag won't catch all the dust from your work but will get most of it. Many modern models are fitted with ports to which you can connect a shop vacuum.

Router. Basically a rotating electric chisel, a router can make quick work of cutting notches and mortises for fence work. It can also add that special decorative touch to posts, rails, and infill.

Table saw. You may not need one of these often, but when it comes to gang-cutting infill for modular fence panels, or making straight rip cuts when trimming infill, nothing works better. Most fencing projects don't take much time, and that means your rental costs will be fairly low.

Power miter saw. This tool is another candidate for rental. It makes quick work of cutting accurate angles. If your fence design includes miter cuts (and most do), you'll want to make them with a power miter saw.

Reciprocating saw. A reciprocating saw is often used in demolition work, but nothing beats it for quickly cutting posts to height.

CORDLESS POWER TOOLS

A novelty when they first appeared on the market, cordless power tools are now used widely throughout the building trades. Potent batteries give these tools surprising power, often allowing you to make hundreds of cuts or holes before recharging.

Battery sizes and configurations are not standard from one manufacturer to the other. If you think you may eventually purchase more than one cordless tool, stick to a single manufacturer and make sure all the tools accept the same battery. This way, you can switch batteries or tools in the middle of a job. Cordless sets are cost-effective—many will include a circular saw, a drill, and a reciprocating saw. Always get at least one extra battery.

CHOOSING MATERIALS

Choosing materials is a balancing act. Consider how you want to use the fence, how you want it to look, how long you want it to last, and how much you can afford to spend on it. Chain link, for example, makes a good, inexpensive, and durable swimming-pool fence, but it won't do much for privacy unless you increase its height and install vinyl inserts. Each material comes with its own strong and not-so-strong points.

Naturally resistant woods

Redwood and cedar offer a high degree of natural resistance to rot and insect damage. They are also more expensive, but have a warm, rich, reddish brown color, and can stand up to the elements. Left untreated these woods will last for years and will age to a rich, deep gray. Ask for heartwood grades—they come from the center of the tree and are more resistant. The lighter colored sapwood is not.

Treated lumber

Pressure-treated (PT) lumber, typically southern pine infused with a chemical preservative, is made for outdoor use and is less expensive than naturally resistant species. Until recently, about 90 percent of the PT wood sold was treated with chromated copper arsenate (CCA), but because of its potential health risk, it began being phased out of residential sales beginning December 31, 2003. You may still see it in your retail outlets—suppliers are allowed to sell the stock they had on hand as of that date.

Alternatives to CCA use safer chemicals—commonly alkaline (or ammoniacal) copper quaternary (ACQ) or copper-azole. ACQ lumber will display a light brown tint, copper azole a light green.

The grade stamp on the board tells when the wood was treated, with which chemical, and for what kinds of uses the wood is rated. Buy PT lumber rated for ground contact for posts and bottom rails—and even for the infill, too (in most cases its bottom edge will be within 6 inches of the ground).

CEDAR

Imported hardwoods

Imported hardwoods, such as Ipe, meranti, teak, Honduran or Central American mahogany, and African mahogany (khaya) will give your outdoor project an exotic look at an exotic price. They will also last almost forever.

Most are extremely hard and may prove difficult to work with—predrilling is a must. Some species won't accept finishes. Others can be finished with hardwood stains or oils. Check with the Certified Forest Products Council (www.certified wood.org) to make sure you're buying from a sustainable forest.

Other native hardwoods, including bald cypress, honey locust, black locust,

REDWOOD

PRESSURE-TREATED WOOD

and sassafras, make excellent fencing–though they're not available in every region.

Synthetic materials

Fences made from synthetic materials, such as vinyl, composites (made from recycled products and resins), and fiberglass-polypropylene formulations, come in a variety of styles that resemble wood and metal varieties. You can get pickets, lattice, boards, basket weaves, and fencing that looks like ornamental metal. Solid infill fences come in prefabricated panels, a few of which require assembly. You can rack some of these styles to follow the contour of a slope, and you can modify end posts to install stepped styles.

Although their lateral and load-bearing strength is not as great as wood or metal, synthetics are otherwise virtually indestructible. Once available only in whites and browns, they now offer an array of colors and don't need painting. Most models are made as kits with posts, rails, and infill cut to the right lengths. Panels are usually 72 to 96 inches long.

Prefabricated wood panels

Prefabricated wood-fence panels go up in a hurry. All you have to do is install posts, nail on the bays, and apply the finish. They may even be less expensive than constructing your own. Many models bear some scrutiny for quality, however.

Examine your prospective choices carefully. An inexpensive product may contain construction shortcuts and cheap materials.

You want panels made with pressure-treated lumber and 2×4 rails assembled with galvanized nails (not staples). Make sure the product is a worthwhile investment that will give you years of service and not require excessive repair.

Metal fences

Tubular aluminum and steel fences are manufactured in many sizes, designs, and

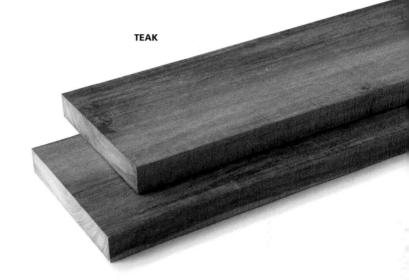

TEAK

colors. They add a touch of elegance to any yard. They're manufactured in kits, most with posts, rails, prefabricated panels (in 72- to 96-inch lengths and various heights), and all the necessary hardware. Some prefab panels are made to be fastened between wooden posts.

If you're fencing a slope, ask your retailer if the style you want can be racked to conform to the contour of the slope. And if your slope is steep, you'll need angled panels.

Not all metal fencing is made with the same quality of materials. Buy the heaviest gauge you can afford–in a color that blends with the character of your home and landscape style. Make sure the finish is a polypowder coating.

Because the panels are precut to a consistent length, these fences require installation one panel at a time–you set one post, then the panel, then the next post, and so on.

Chain link is the other metal choice for fencing. It's inexpensive, easy to install, and a higher quality material that reduces maintenance. Buy the heaviest gauge you can afford. The cost will pay you back in durability. Chain link is not the most attractive material, but a vinyl coating will dress things up a bit. So will colored inserts.

Lumber grades

Lumber is graded according to the quality of its surface. Various manufacturing associations and different woods have different systems, but the following is a general synthesis of all of them.

■ **Clear.** Has no knots.

■ **Select.** High-quality wood. Select board grades are B and better, C, and D. Select structural is the top grade in dimension lumber.

■ **No. 2 common.** Boards with tight knots and no major blemishes.

■ **No. 3 common.** Knots in these boards may be loose; board may be blemished or damaged.

■ **Standard.** Middle-grade framing lumber; good strength; used for general framing.

■ **Utility.** Economy grade used for rough framing.

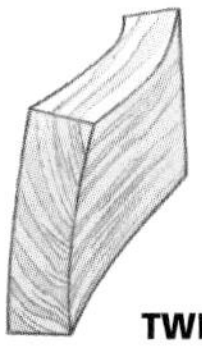

Inspecting boards

If you order lumber by telephone, you will get someone else's choice of boards, not your own. Lumberyards usually have lots of substandard wood lying around; the only way to be sure you do not get some of it is to pick out each board yourself. Some lumberyards will not allow you to sort through their inventory because they want to keep wood neatly stacked—the best way to keep lumber from warping. But they should at least let you stand by and approve the selection. If not, confirm that you can return boards you don't like. Here are some lumber flaws to watch for:

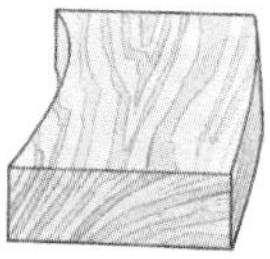

■ A board that is heavily twisted, bowed, cupped, or crooked usually is not usable, although some bows will lie down as you nail them in place.

TWIST

BOW

LUMBER SIZES

■ **Furring.** Rough wood of small dimensions for trim, shimming, stakes, light-duty frames, latticework, and edging.

Nominal size	Actual size
1×2	¾ ×1½ "
1×3	¾ ×2½ "

■ **Boards.** Smooth-finished lumber for general construction, trimwork, and decking.

Nominal size	Actual size
1×4	¾ × 3½ "
1×6	¾ × 5½ "
1×8	¾ × 7¼ "
1×10	¾ × 9¼ "
1×12	¾ × 11¼ "

■ For fencing, you'll need 4×4 or 6×6 posts, 2×4s for rails, 2×6s for cap rails, and 1× stock for infill.

■ **Dimension lumber.** Studs are usually 2×4, sometimes 2×6. Planks are 6 inches wide or wider. Use for structural framing, structural finishing, forming, decking, and fencing.

Nominal size	Actual size
2×2	1½ × 1½ "
2×3	1½ × 2½ "
2×4	1½ × 3½ "
2×6	1½ × 5½ "
2×8	1½ × 7¼ "
2×10	1½ × 9¼ "
2×12	1½ × 11¼ "
4×4	3½ × 3½ "
4×6	3½ × 5½ "
6×6	5½ × 5½ "

CUP

KNOTS

■ Knots are only a cosmetic problem unless they are loose and likely to pop out.

■ Checking, which is a rift in the surface, is only cosmetic.

■ Splits cannot be repaired and will widen in time. Cut off split ends.

CHECKS

SPLITS

Nominal dimensions

Nominal dimensions, such as 2×4 or 1×6, are used when buying lumber. Keep in mind that the actual dimensions of the lumber will be less, as indicated in the table, opposite. Lumber prices are often calculated by the board foot– the equivalent of a piece 12 nominal inches square and 1 nominal inch thick. Most lumberyards will not require you to calculate board feet, but if you want to, here's the formula: Multiply thickness by width, both in nominal inches and by length in feet, then divide by 12. Example: 2×4, 8 feet long: 2×4×8=64; 64/12=5.33 bd. ft.

READING A GRADE STAMP

Grade stamps at one end of a board provide important information about the lumber: its species, whether it's heartwood or sapwood, whether it has been pressure treated (and, if so, with what chemical), and whether it's suitable for contact with the ground.

■ Plywood, marked on the face of the sheet, is rated by the American Plywood Association (APA). For outdoor projects, insist on exterior-grade plywood, which resists weathering better than interior grades, or pressure-treated material.

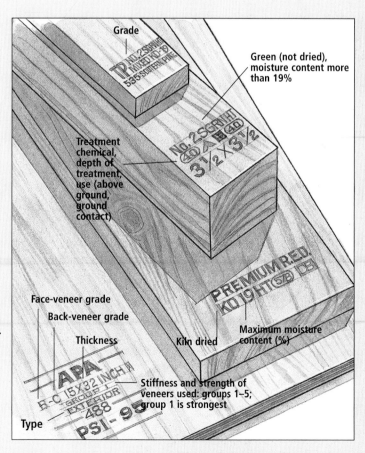

FASTENERS AND HARDWARE

Just as important as the quality of the lumber that goes into your fence is the quality of the fasteners that will hold it together. Whatever outdoor fasteners and hardware you choose, make sure they are rustproof–galvanized or stainless steel, brass, or other rust-resistant metal.

Nails

Once sold for so many pennies per hundred, nails today are sold by the pound. But nails still are described and sized by this old terminology; for example, a 16-penny or a 4-penny nail. To further complicate things, "penny" is indicated by the letter *d* (probably for *denarius*, Latin for *coin*). What really matters is the length of the nail (in most cases, the thickness of a nail follows its length). (See the chart, opposite, to translate pennyweight into inches.)

Just as there are many sizes of nails, there are many types of nail shank. Each has a different holding power. Ringshank and spiral-shank nails grip the wood fibers better than smooth (common or box) nails and don't easily work their way out. In fact they can be difficult to remove.

Of all the sizes and shapes available, these nails work well for most fence projects:

Common or **ringshank nails** (16d) for the frame–in 2× or thicker stock.

Box or **ringshank nails** (8d or 10d) for the infill–in 1× or thinner stock.

Finishing nails (6d or 8d) for the fine trim.

Duplex nails for temporary fasteners; they have a double head, which makes them easy to pull out when you strip away forms or braces, for example.

For small jobs, buy nails in 1-pound boxes or in bulk quantities by the pound. Keep an assortment of brads on hand. Brads look like miniature finishing nails; use them for molding and finishing jobs.

Screws

Screws hold better than nails and come in a multitude of styles. They're also easy to remove, which makes correcting mistakes easier. Your fence construction will require deck screws–usually in 2½- to 3½-inch lengths. Deck screws are coated to resist the elements and are sharp, tapered, and self-sinking. You can drive them

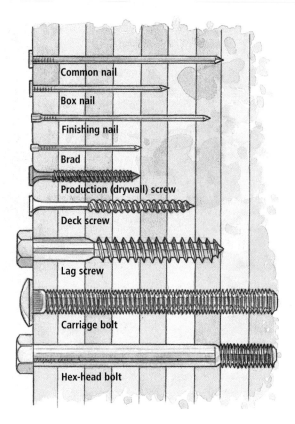

Common nail
Box nail
Finishing nail
Brad
Production (drywall) screw
Deck screw
Lag screw
Carriage bolt
Hex-head bolt

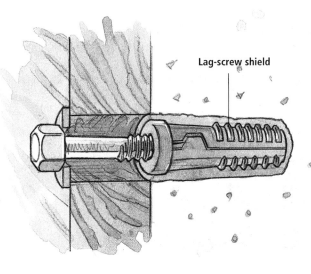

Lag-screw shield

METAL BRACKETS

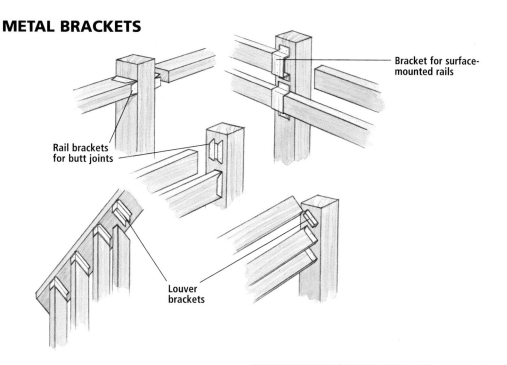

Bracket for surface-mounted rails

Rail brackets for butt joints

Louver brackets

with a cordless drill about as quickly as you can hammer nails.

Regardless of the size you use, predrill holes when driving them within 2 inches of the end of a board. This keeps the wood from splitting. Use a drill bit the same size as the screw shank (not the threads).

Screw heads vary in style and slot type. You need phillips, square-drive, or combination heads. Get square-drive heads if possible. They tend to strip out less than phillips-head screws.

A **lag screw** is a large screw with a hexagonal head used to secure heavy framing members and hardware. Tighten them with a wrench.

Bolts and brackets

Bolts, nuts, and washers provide a solid connection with excellent load-bearing strength. Use only zinc-coated or stainless-steel ones. Drill holes with a bit of the same diameter. Bolts are sized by length, diameter, and threads per inch. For example, a ½-13×3-inch bolt is ½ inch in diameter, has 13 threads per inch, and is 3 inches long.

Metal fence brackets work well for quick installations and solid connections. Brackets can join rails to posts, prefabricated fence bays to posts, and louvered boards to posts (horizontal louvers) or rails (vertical louvers).

SIZING NAILS AND SCREWS

What size nail or screw will you need for the job? A fastener that's too small won't hold; one that's too big risks splitting the material or poking through the material to which you are fastening.

■ Use this table to convert nail pennies (d) into inches:

3d = 1¼"	4d = 1½"	6d = 2"
7d = 2¼"	8d = 2½"	10d = 3"
12d = 3¼"	16d = 3½"	20d = 4"

■ Select nails three times as long as the thickness of the material you are fastening. For instance, to attach a 1×4 (¾ inch thick), a 6d nail (2 inches long) will be a bit short. An 8d nail (2½ inches), a little more than three times the thickness of the 1×4, will do better. If the nail is so long it would go through the base material, use a screw.

■ Screws are sized by their length and gauge (diameter). The length of the screw, in inches, should be shorter than the thickness of the materials into which it will be driven. The smooth shank of a screw should go through the top material being fastened.

■ The gauge of screws you will need for a given project depends on the fastening strength required. Designated by number, gauges range from No. 0, which has a diameter of ¹⁄₁₆ inch, to No. 20, which is nearly ½ inch in diameter.

MEASURING AND MARKING

SQUARING UP STOCK

Mark and cut board square

Before you measure or fasten any board, make sure its end is square. Check it with a try square, layout square, or combination square, as shown. Mark the edge and cut it with a circular saw or miter saw.

MARKING CROSSCUTS

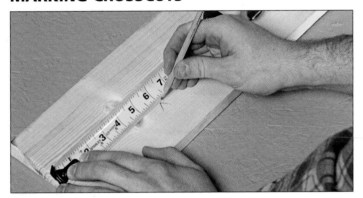

1 Mark the cut point with a "V." A dot is too difficult to see, and a short line might veer one way or the other. Always double-check your measurement before making any cuts.

2 Set the blade of a combination square or layout square on the "V" mark and extend the measurement to both edges of the board. For wide stock, line up a framing square to mark the cutoff line.

Even the simplest fence will require a variety of measuring tools. The most common is probably going to be your tape measure. Get into the habit of starting each job by clipping a steel tape to your belt.

There's an old carpenter's adage that says "measure twice, cut once." It's been around for years with good reason–it's amazingly easy to misread a measurement, even if you're a pro. Don't take anything for granted when measuring; mistakes waste time and material.

You'll need a sharp-pointed pencil to make accurate marks on your material. Carpenter's pencils, which have flat rather than round leads, work well for marking wood. For even more accuracy, use an awl, which looks like a short ice pick, or a scriber, which resembles a long steel toothpick.

Although you may make most rip cuts with a table saw, if you use a circular saw, equip it with a rip-cutting guide and make sure the guide does not wander off the edge of the board.

SAW ON SCRAP SIDE

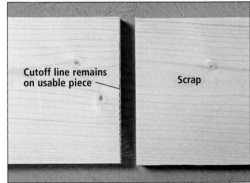

Cutoff line remains on usable piece

Scrap

Saw on the scrap side of the cutoff line, not straight down the middle of it. Otherwise your board will be half a saw kerf shorter than the length you want. Even this small discrepancy—typically 1/16 inch—can make a big difference.

Using squares and levels

Square refers to an exact 90-degree angle between two surfaces. When a material is level, it's perfectly horizontal; when it's plumb, it's truly vertical.

Never assume that existing construction is square, level, or plumb. It probably isn't. To prove this to yourself, lay a level horizontally along any floor in your home, hold a level vertically against a wall section in a corner, or place a square on a door or window frame. Don't be alarmed at the results. Variation is normal because houses and other structures settle slightly on their foundations, throwing off square, level, and plumb.

How can you check a level's accuracy? Lay it on a horizontal surface and shim it, if necessary, to get a level reading. Then turn the level end for end. If you don't get the same reading, the level needs to be adjusted or replaced. Some models allow you to calibrate the level by rotating the glass vials. Laser levels (see page 99) come with instructions for their calibration.

MARKING ANGLES

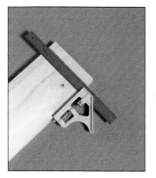 

Use a combination square, layout square, or bevel gauge to mark angles. A combination square and layout square can make only 45- and 90-degree angles. A bevel gauge can allow you to duplicate any angle and transfer it to the surface you're cutting.

USING A FRAMING SQUARE

For large squaring jobs, use a framing square, setting it on the inside or outside of the corner as the framing allows.

USING A POST LEVEL

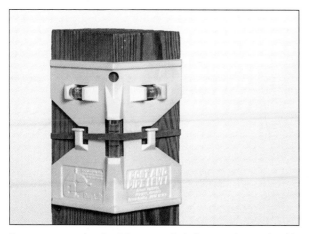

Fence posts must be plumb in two vertical planes, and a post level is made specifically for this job. Strap the level about halfway up the final length of the post. Adjust the post until all three bubbles are centered in their vials.

USING A CARPENTER'S LEVEL

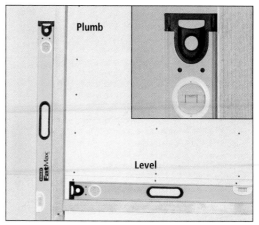

The longer the level, the more precise your alignments will be. Use a 4-foot carpenter's level unless you don't have room. Use the end vials to plumb a board, the center vial to check for level.

USING A CIRCULAR SAW

Most circular saws come with a combination blade that will make crosscuts and rip cuts equally well. If yours is equipped with a standard steel blade, replace it with a carbide-toothed combination blade. To change the blade on your saw, unplug it and retract the blade guard. Set the teeth of the blade firmly into the top of your outside work surface. Remove the bolt and tilt the blade out. Reverse the procedure to replace the blade.

Set the blade so it extends no more than ¼ inch (about 3 teeth) through the thickness of the stock. Release the saw plate latch to position the blade to the proper depth. For all cuts, start the saw off the cut and push the blade into the board with a fairly rapid, constant forward motion.

Cutting lumber, especially pressure-treated stock, calls for protection. Protect your eyes from flying chips and sawdust with safety glasses. If you are sensitive to pressure-treated lumber, use a face mask. When making frequent cuts, wear ear protectors.

CUTTING FREEHAND

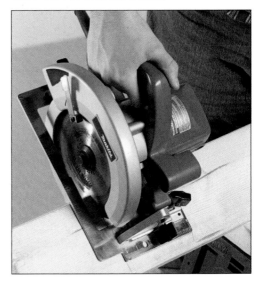

Making freehand cuts will save you a lot of time, but they might take a little practice. Set the edge of the board on a solid surface and hold it at a 30- to 45-degree angle. Line up the saw guide with your cut line, start the saw, and let gravity pull it down the line. Keep the saw plate flat on the stock as you cut.

CROSSCUTTING WITH A GUIDE

With the saw plate flat on the board and the saw guide lined up with the waste side of the cut line, clamp a layout square against the edge of the saw plate. Start the saw and push it forward. With practice you can dispense with the clamp and hold the square with your other hand.

RIP CUTTING

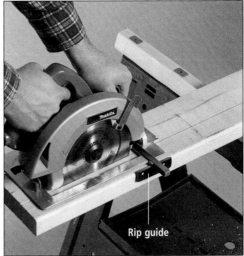

Rip guide

Narrow rip cuts are easy to make with a rip guide. Line up the saw guide with the cut line and tighten the rip guide. Don't force the saw—the rip guide might flex off the line. For angled rip cuts, clamp a long straightedge to the board and use it as a guide.

CUTTING MITERS

You can cut miters freehand, but a layout square and a clamp will give you a straight cut. Clamp the board to a solid surface. Retract the blade guard before starting the saw and don't push too hard. Cut the miter before you trim the length of the board—that way you can try again if you make a mistake.

CUTTING BEVELS

Bevel gauge

Like miter cuts, bevels are a two-handed job. Clamp the board firmly to a work surface and clamp a layout square to the board so the blade will cut on the waste side of the line. Set the bevel gauge to the correct angle and check it with a protractor. Start the saw and ease it into the cut with a slow but constant speed.

CUTTING POSTS

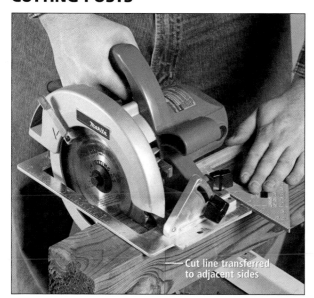

Cut line transferred to adjacent sides

To get a level cut when you cut your posts, you'll need to mark the cut line on all four sides. First mark the cut line on one face of the post and transfer the mark to the adjoining sides with a layout square. Then cut the post with a circular saw or reciprocating saw.

Keep saw shoe against wood throughout the cut.

Use a blade long enough to cut through stock.

Set a circular saw with the blade to the waste side of the line and cut each adjacent side. When using a reciprocating saw, keep the shoe against the post so the saw won't kick back.

Using a Table Saw and Power Miter Saw

You can build a fence without a table saw or a power miter saw, but there are many things these saws can do faster and more accurately than a circular saw. Nothing can beat them for ripping long boards, making notches and dadoes, or cutting clean, accurate mitered corners in your top rail.

Both table saw and miter saw blades need periodic checking to make sure they are square to their tables. A blade that's out of square will produce an unintended bevel cut.

For a table saw, turn the blade up to its limit and set the tilt scale to 0 degrees. Place one side of a square on the table and the other against the blade, between the teeth. Turn the tilt control until there is no gap between the square and the blade, then lock the stop screw. Level a miter saw table with a torpedo level.

Power saws are dangerous. Avoid cutting warped wood; it's more likely to kick back. Stand to one side of a table saw blade, not directly behind it. Extend a table saw blade a maximum of ¼ inch above the thickness of the work—more blade means more risk of kickback. On any table saw cut narrower than 5 inches, use a push stick. It will keep your hands higher than the blade. Attach your miter saw to a waist-high work surface and keep one hand on the trigger and the other on the work. Wear ear and eye protection when using either saw.

MAKING RIP CUTS

Feather board keeps stock tightly against fence.

Nothing makes rip cuts more precisely and easier than a table saw. First lock the rip-fence guide at the width of the cut. Then set the board (good side up) on the table, snug against the fence. Turn the saw on and feed the work steadily into the blade and completely past it, using a push stick at the end of any cut less than 5 inches wide. Turn off the power and when the blade stops spinning, remove the boards.

CUTTING MITERS

To cut miters, first mark the cut line on the board (so you can see that the cut is correct) and set the miter gauge at the same angle. Raise the saw blade so the teeth are ¼ inch above the stock and line up the waste side of the cut with the right edge of the blade. Turn the power on and feed the stock slowly into and completely beyond the blade.

CROSSCUTTING WITH A TABLE SAW

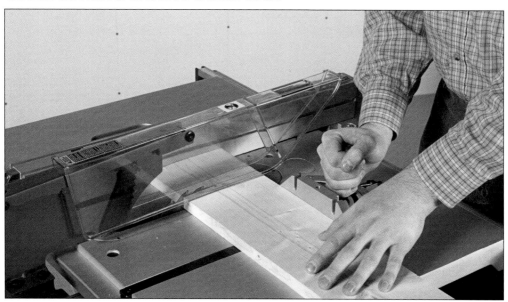

To make a crosscut with a table saw, position the rip fence so it won't touch the end of the board. Set the board on the table and raise the blade so the teeth are ¼ inch above the top surface. Set the board with a true edge squarely in the miter gauge and back about an inch from the blade. Turn the power on. Hold the board securely in the miter gauge and push it smoothly into and completely beyond the blade. Shut the power off and remove the stock when the blade stops spinning.

USING A POWER MITER SAW

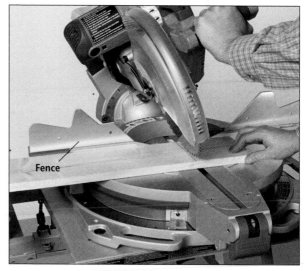

To cut miters on a power miter saw, first mark the cut line on the board and set it square against the fence. Lower the blade just above the board and position the board so the cut line is about ¹⁄₁₆ inch from the blade. Hold the board with one hand, and with the other, squeeze the trigger. Let the saw come to full speed and lower the blade into the work. Reposition the work and make successive cuts to the cut line.

To cut bevels, set the miter scale at the angle of the cut and lock it. Then lock the blade at the angle of the bevel. Holding the board firmly against the fence, lower the blade and position the board directly under it. Then raise the saw, start the saw, and bring it to full speed. Lower the blade slowly and cut completely through the stock. Let the blade come to rest before removing the cut piece.

FASTENING

here's a basic set of skills associated with fastening tools, but it doesn't take long to master them.

Using a hammer

For maximum leverage and control, hold the hammer near the end of the handle. Grasp the nail near its head and lightly tap it until it stands by itself. Keep your eye on the nail as you swing the hammer, letting its weight do the driving. With the last hammer blow, set the head of the nail flush with the surface of the wood. The convex shape of the hammer face allows you to do this without marring the surface of the wood.

Using a cordless drill

When driving screws with a cordless drill, set the clutch so it disengages when the screw head is flush with the wood. To drive a screw, hold it with one hand and give it a couple of turns with the drill until it sets itself in the wood. Keep the screwdriver tip square to the head and firmly in the recess. Start slowly with moderate pressure on the drill, increasing both the speed of the drill and the pressure until the screw is driven home.

DRIVING NAILS

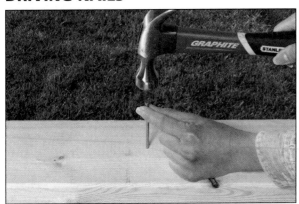

Hold the nail near its head. That way if you miss, the hammer will glance off your fingers rather than crush them.

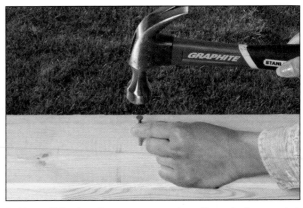

To hit a nail dead-on, keep your eye on the nail, not the hammer. Let the weight of the hammer do the work. You don't need to apply a lot of muscle to it. After a while you'll find you can sink a nail in just three or four blows.

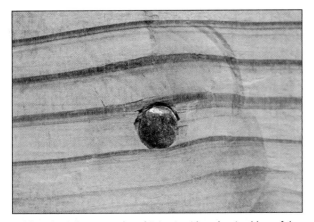

Holding the nail at an angle or hitting it with a glancing blow of the hammer will cut the wood fibers as you drive the nail home. Over-seating the nail will create a pocket that will hold water.

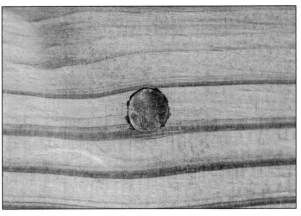

Hitting the nail head squarely with the hammer will avoid cut wood fibers. With the final blow of the hammer, set the nail head so it just dents the surface.

FACENAILING

Skewed nails will increase their hold in the wood, especially when driven into end grain. Drive in one nail at a 60-degree angle in one direction, then drive in another nail in the opposite direction. Skewed nails make it difficult for the board to pull loose.

When two framing members meet on top of a post, join them with a scarf joint, centered on the post. Drive two fasteners on either side of the joint. A scarf joint adds visual interest and strength.

Minimize splits, especially at the end of a board, by staggering the nails so they don't fall on the same grain lines. Predrill the nails for added insurance against splits.

To fasten a through-rail (one without a joint) to a post, drive two nails, offsetting them as shown. More nails won't make the joint stronger and could split the wood.

TOENAILING

Nailing near the end of a board tends to split the wood. To avoid this problem when toenailing, blunt the tip of the nail or drill a pilot hole first.

To toenail a rail to a post, hold the nail at a steep angle, tap it once or twice, then reduce the angle to 45 degrees as you drive the nail home.

PREDRILLING AND DRIVING SCREWS

Using a drill bit whose diameter is the same size as the shaft of the screw (not the threads), drill a hole at the angle of the fastener. Push the tip of the screw slightly into the hole and drive the screw, keeping the drill in line with the angle of the screw and pressed firmly into the screw head.

Overdriving a screw beyond the surface of the wood creates a pocket that can trap water. Use a cordless drill and set its clutch to release just when the screw is flush with the surface of the wood.

 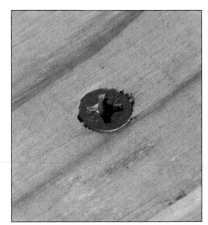

COUNTERBORING

Spade bit same diameter as socket wrench

Bore ⅛" deeper than thickness of bolt head or nut.

Twist drill bit same diameter as bolt shank

Lag screws and machine bolts look better with countersunk heads. To counterbore a hole, start with a spade bit the same diameter as your washer. Drill a hole ⅛ inch deeper than the thickness of the head or nut and wide enough for a socket wrench.

Using a twist drill bit the same diameter as the bolt, drill completely through the stock. Slide the bolt through washers and use washers under the nut too. Caulk the recess with silicone.

FASTENER LENGTH

To make sure your fastened joints are strong and secure, use a fastener that penetrates into the bottom board by about two-thirds of the thickness of that board.

LAG SCREWS AND BOLTS

Like other screws, lag screws require a pilot hole the same diameter as the shank of the screw. Bolts require a hole bored through the pieces being joined.

Machine bolts

Machine bolts have hexagonal heads and threads running partway or all the way along the shank. When fastening two pieces of wood together, slip a flat washer onto the bolt and slide the bolt through the holes in both pieces of material. Add another flat washer, then a lock washer. The flat washer keeps the nut and the bolt head from digging into the wood. The lock washer prevents the nut from coming loose. Use two wrenches—one to hold the bolt and the other to draw the nut down onto the bolt.

Countersunk bolts

Use a socket wrench to install a machine bolt in a place that's hard to reach or when the bolt head is countersunk into a hole in the wood.

Carriage bolts

A carriage bolt has a plain, round head. Insert it into the hole and tap the bottom face of the head flush with the surface. No washer is needed under the head. The square or hexagonal shoulder under the head keeps the bolt from spinning as the nut is tightened.

Slip a flat washer, a lock washer, and a nut onto the bolt. Tighten the nut. The lock washer will keep the nut from working loose.

MACHINE BOLT

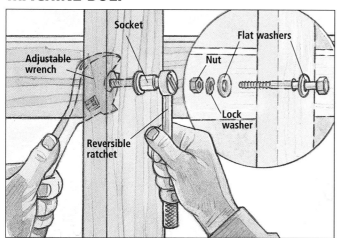

COUNTERSUNK BOLT

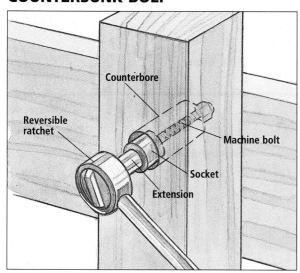

CARRIAGE BOLT

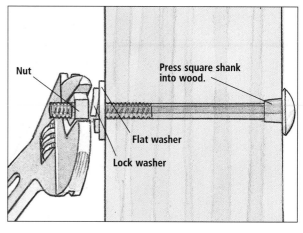

MAKING LATTICE PANELS

Latticework adds grace to a fence, makes an excellent privacy and windscreen, and creates peek-through panels that roses and climbing vines can't resist.

Before you buy materials, sketch a cross-section of the frame and decide how thick you want the lattice. Using ¾-inch lattice will give you a sturdy, long-lasting structure, but the combined thickness of a 2×2 frame and two layers of ¾-inch lattice will be 3½ inches–the same as the width of the 2×4 rails. Trimming the edges will mean that the trim sticks out ¾ inch beyond the rails. If this creates the look you want, there's not a problem. If you don't like the way this looks, you can leave the frame untrimmed, buy thinner lattice, or use trim wide enough to cover the gap between the frame and the rail.

■ Begin by building a 2×2 frame to fit exactly between your posts. Measure the space between the posts at the top and bottom. The width may vary a bit if the posts aren't plumb.

■ Painting is easier before the lattice is assembled. Paint assembled lattice with a roller or sprayer and touch up edges with a brush.

■ Use 3d galvanized box nails to fasten the lattice to the frame. Their surfaces grip the wood securely and provide rust resistance. You'll need a half pound of 3d nails to assemble a 4×8-foot lattice frame.

■ After attaching the lath to the frame, use a straightedge or chalk line to mark across the top and bottom of the lattice panel, flush with the outer edge of the frame. Double-check to make sure no edges of nailheads will be in the path of the saw.

■ Trim the lattice with a circular saw or a handsaw. If you are using a circular saw, adjust it to cut no deeper than the layers of lath, as shown in the inset illustration for Step 5. With a handsaw, you should be able to just graze the edge of the frame as you trim. Use a fine-tooth blade for easy cutting and a smooth edge. Sand off any saw marks on the frame.

KEEP LATTICE FRAMEWORK SQUARE

When you build a fence frame for a lattice-paneled project, brace and plumb each post and set it in concrete. To provide more rigidity, run horizontal and diagonal stringers (2×4s) across the posts. Assemble the lattice frames and install them between the posts, then remove the stringers.

LATTICE PANELS: STEP-BY-STEP

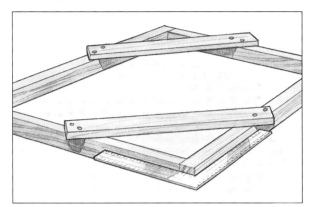

1 To keep the frame straight while you are working, tack scraps of wood diagonally to the back. Turn the frame over when you fasten the nailers and lattice strips. Then remove the braces.

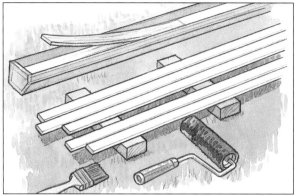

2 The quickest way to paint lattice is by dipping the strips in paint before you fasten them to the frame. A length of 4-inch rain gutter capped at both ends makes an ideal dipping tank. Or lay the lath across scraps of wood and paint it with a roller.

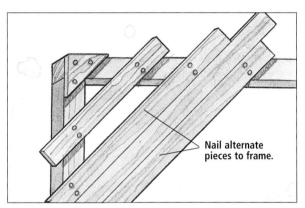

Nail alternate pieces to frame.

3 To assemble the lattice panel, fasten the first strip of lath to the frame. Then, using a second strip as a spacer, fit and fasten the third strip. Repeat this process until you have covered the frame. Then assemble the second layer, placing the strips at right angles to the first layer.

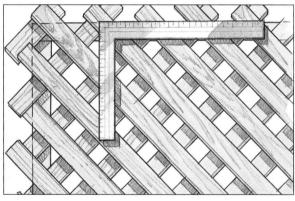

4 After attaching the lath to the frame, mark the lattice so you can trim it flush with the outside edge of the frame. Use a chalk line or straightedge for accuracy.

Saw blade just clears lath thickness

5 After solidly positioning the panel on sawhorses or another raised base, cut both layers of lattice flush with the frame.

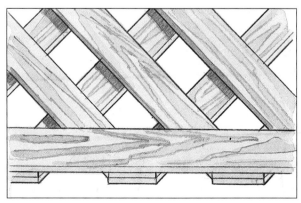

6 Trim the edges of the lattice using lath strips with mitered corners.

LAYING OUT YOUR FENCE AND SETTING POSTS

L aying out a fence line is the first, and perhaps the most critical, step in constructing a fence. Do this one right and the rest of your construction will go smoothly.

The illustrations on these pages show the essential steps in locating and lining up your posts. Before you start, check with the city or county zoning office to make sure your project will comply with building codes and ordinances regarding setback from your property line. Most locations have a single phone number you can call to have the buried pipes and wires on your property located and marked before you dig. Your local electric utility can probably provide the number. If you can't find the number, call the North American One-Call Referral System at 888-258-0808.

1 Build batterboards from 2×4s by fastening crosspieces to the "legs" and driving them into the ground 3 to 4 feet beyond the ends of your fence line. Drive another pair of batterboards perpendicular to the first pair and parallel to the house, property line, or whatever plane in your landscape you will use to locate the fence. Tie mason's line to each pair of batterboards, pulling the line tight.

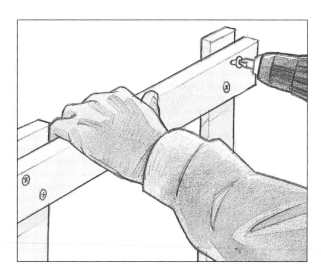

2 Starting at the intersection of the lines, measure 3 feet (or a multiple of three) out on one line and mark that point with a piece of tape. Measure 4 feet (or a multiple) on the other line and mark it. Measure the distance between the pieces of tape. If the diagonal measures 5 feet (or a multiple), the corner is square, and the fence line will be perpendicular to the house or other plane of reference. If necessary, adjust the lines until they make a 5-foot diagonal. Mark the final position of the lines on the crosspieces.

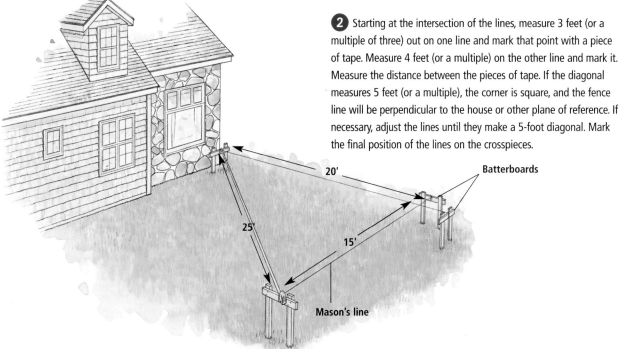

20'

25'

15'

Batterboards

Mason's line

Get organized

You'll need several pieces of equipment to lay out a fence line. To visualize the layout, use a tape measure and a garden hose to outline its dimensions on the ground. Then gather and cut the lumber for the batterboards. You will need a small sledge hammer to drive the batterboards into the ground, a cordless drill/driver, a plumb bob, a camera tripod, a spool of mason's line, and deck screws to assemble them.

From there on, you'll need a posthole digger, shovel, level, hammer, circular saw for cutting posts to length, a tamping rod or board, and, if you're mixing your own concrete, a wheelbarrow or mixing box and a concrete hoe.

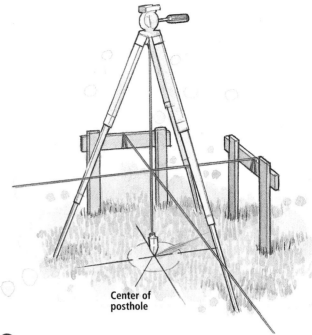

Center of posthole

3 At each intersection drop a plumb bob to mark the location of the center of the post. Drive a stake or landscaping nail where the plumb bob comes to rest. Then move the plumb bob down the fence line to your next post location and mark its center with the same technique. Continue staking the post centers until you have marked all of them.

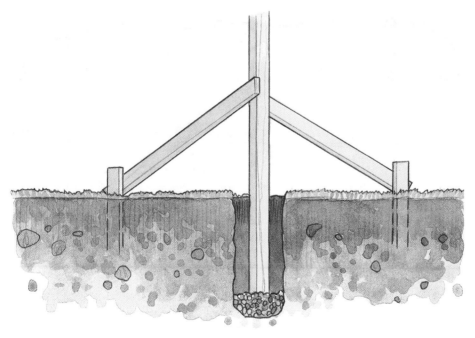

4 Remove the mason's lines from the batterboards (to get them out of your way). Then dig the postholes and shovel 3 inches of gravel into each one. The gravel lets water drain away from the bottom of the post and reduces the opportunities for rot. Set the post on the gravel and support it with temporary braces.

In general, and in most areas of the country, posts anchored in concrete are the best way to support a fence or gate. However, in some areas of the country (notably in frost-free regions), and in some soils, you can set the posts in a tamped earth-and-gravel base. Your local building codes may have something to say about setting posts, so check with your building department before digging the holes.

Define each corner with a pair of batterboards. For each batterboard make a pair of stakes by cutting a point on one end of two 2×4s. Attach a crossbar (see Step 1) and drive the batterboards into the ground 3 to 4 feet outside the planned corner location. Locate them so that a line connecting the posthole centerlines will be at about the center of the crossbar.

However you decide to set your posts, be sure to dig holes for them 6 inches deeper than the frost line in your area to counter the effects of frost heaving. Dig an 8-inch-diameter hole for each 4×4 post, using a power auger, hand auger, or posthole digger (see pages 96–97). A 6×6 post requires a 10-inch-diameter hole.

Concrete choices

Unless you are constructing an extremely long fence, consider using premixed bags of

Snap level chalk line at the height of posts and cut them with a reciprocating saw.

Braces

Outside post face just touches mason's line or is set ⅛ inch inside the line.

1x2 stake

5 Replace the mason's lines on the batterboards—only this time, tie them to the outside of your original marks at a point equal to half the thickness of your posts (1¾ inches for 4-inch posts). Now the mason's lines will represent the outside faces of the posts. With a helper and working on one post at a time, loosen the temporary braces, plumb each post on two sides, and rebrace it with its outside face just touching the line. If you're concerned that the posts may push the line out of place, set each post a consistent ⅛ inch inside the lines.

concrete. They come with the correct amount of sand and gravel added to the cement; all you do is add water and mix. Premixed bags also make it easier for you to set some of the posts on one day and come back the next day to set the rest of them, without having your work schedule dictated by unused concrete.

You can, of course, buy the cement in bags, order sand and gravel, and mix the concrete yourself. Mixing it yourself is less expensive, but the convenience of premixed concrete is usually worth the extra money. In either case you will need gravel for the bottom of the postholes.

Mixing concrete
For most post-setting projects, mix three parts gravel with two parts sand and one part cement.

If you mix your own concrete, move the mixing container as close to your posts as possible. That way you won't have to haul concrete across the yard in a wheelbarrow.

The amount of water needed depends on how wet the sand is. You'll need less water with wet sand than with dry sand. Test the wetness by squeezing some sand in your hand. If water seeps out, the sand is too wet. If the ball compacts like moist clay, the sand is too dry. As you mix the concrete, add very small amounts of water at a time. When it becomes one color—medium gray—and sticks slightly to a shovel held almost at 90 degrees, it's ready.

Once the concrete has cured, mark the height of the posts and cut them with a reciprocating saw (see illustration, opposite).

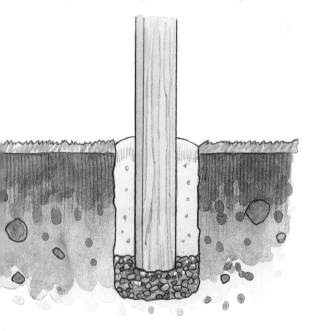

6 Add about 2 inches more gravel around the post. Mix and pour in concrete, tamping it as you fill to remove air bubbles. Slope the concrete around the top of the hole to drain away water that might cause rot. After the concrete sets, remove the braces.

7 For a watertight seal around posts in concrete, apply silicone caulk around the post base after the concrete cures. That way, even if a post shrinks a bit over time, it will be protected against rot.

Although setting posts in concrete is the most common method of anchoring them, there are a couple of alternatives. In some localities you can dig the holes and set the posts in tamped earth and gravel. And with a drive-in post anchor like the one shown below right, you don't even have to dig holes.

Setting posts in tamped earth and gravel

As with posts set in concrete, dig holes deep enough to go 6 inches below the frost line, then place several inches of gravel in the bottom of the holes. Posts in shallow holes or without the gravel can easily be knocked out of plumb.

Set a post in place, plumb it, and brace it with diagonal braces as shown on page 124. Then shovel about 4 inches of soil into the hole on all sides of the post and tamp it firmly. (A length of 2×4 makes a good tamper.) Follow this layer with a 4-inch layer of tamped gravel, alternating the earth and gravel until you've filled the hole. Then mound and tamp the soil around the base of the post; sloping the soil lets water drain away from the post and minimizes chances for rot. After several rainfalls, check the slope. If it has settled, rebuild it and firmly compact it.

Anchoring posts to a patio or deck

If you're building a fence along the edge of an existing patio, deck, or porch, metal post bases will provide you with a handy answer to the question, "How do I anchor them?" Some post bases, such as the one shown opposite, are made to be embedded in wet concrete. Others

SETTING POSTS IN TAMPED EARTH AND GRAVEL

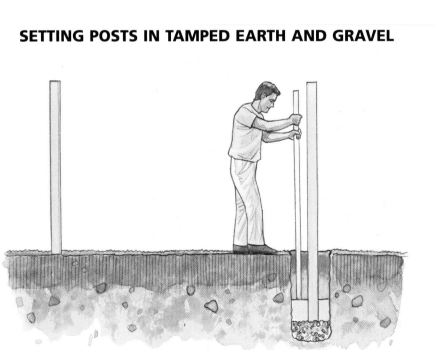

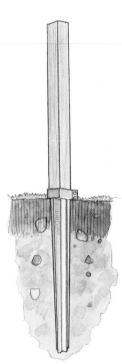

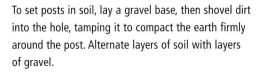
To set posts in soil, lay a gravel base, then shovel dirt into the hole, tamping it to compact the earth firmly around the post. Alternate layers of soil with layers of gravel.

One type of anchor, the GroundTech post installation device, shown above, drives into the ground without digging. You tighten two bolts on the steel fixture to clamp the post into its collar.

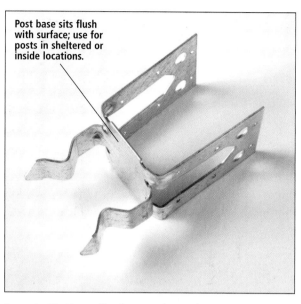

Post base sits flush with surface; use for posts in sheltered or inside locations.

Attach a post to an existing wood or concrete surface with one of these bases. For new work you can embed an anchor bolt for the base when you pour the concrete. These bases provide a 1-inch standoff from the surface and are adjustable so you can correct minor errors in your layout.

Set embedded bases like the ones shown above into the concrete immediately after you pour your footing. They must be accurately positioned to begin with—once the concrete has set, there's no moving them.

fasten to bolts in new or existing concrete. Some of these are adjustable and raise the bottom of the post about 1 inch off the concrete, which keeps the foot of the post above ground moisture and puddled water, reducing the risk of rot.

To install a bolt in existing concrete, drill a hole in the concrete, then inject epoxy cement into the hole with a syringe (which comes with the epoxy). Set the bolt so that the end extends about ¾ inch above the surface.

After the epoxy cures, secure the base with a nut and washer. Then position the post in the base and nail or screw it in place.

You can also use metal anchors to join posts to another wooden structure, such as a deck or porch. Just nail or screw the base to the surface. A simple U-shape base will work where no moisture protection is necessary.

Anchor answers
When building and anchoring a structure, keep these points in mind:
■ Check building codes for local requirements.
■ Don't build a fence on an existing patio or deck without attaching one end to the house, permanent structure, or post embedded in the ground. Ideally a deck or patio fence should be securely anchored at both ends.
■ Always use the fasteners specified for the base.

Laying Out a Curved Fence Line

Curved fences increase the attractiveness of a fence line and can solve some tricky layout problems. They can skirt trees, large rocks, and other obstructions or they can soften corners where you want to avoid feeling cramped.

Curved fences have some structural limitations, however. They're difficult to construct between post spans shorter than 4 feet or longer than 6 feet, they need at least three posts, and the infill has to be narrow, especially in tight curves. Even if you drew the curve precisely on your final plan, you may need to change it to fit the realities of the actual location.

When you set the posts, note their orientation; for most infill styles, the post faces should fall on the arc line.

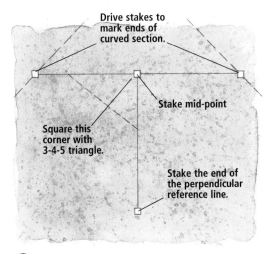

1 Begin your layout by driving stakes at both ends of the curve. Then tie a tight line between them. Drive a stake at the midpoint of that line and extend a perpendicular line to a stake that will serve as the end of your "compass line."

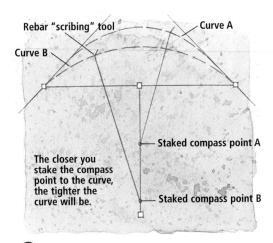

2 Drive a pipe, landscape spike, or stake on the compass line at the point where you want to center the curve. Note that the placement of this "compass point" will determine the depth of the arc and the radius of the curve. Loop one end of a length of mason's line around the center point and tie a short piece of ½-inch rebar to the other end. Scribe the arc of your curve in the ground with the rebar.

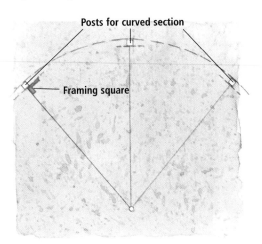

3 Mark each post location on the arc you scribed and dig the holes. Set the posts in each hole and brace them. Run the mason's line from the compass point to the post and use a framing square to make sure the post is perpendicular to the line.

DEALING WITH OBSTACLES

When you're planning your fence and discover that your proposed fence line is going to pass through tree trunks, large rocks, or gullies and other depressions, don't give up. You have more solutions than you might think. You can skirt obstructions such as trees and free-standing boulders by building a circular fence section around them. Other obstructions, for which skirting won't work, call for specialized but remarkably uncomplicated solutions, as illustrated here.

Dealing with trees requires some special considerations. It is usually not a good idea to nail fencing to the trunk of a tree. Puncture wounds can expose a living tree to bacterial invasions and disturb the flow of water and nutrients. Posts can harm a root system if you set them too close to a tree. Reposition the fence line or stop it short of the tree on either side as illustrated so the tree can continue to grow. Bring the fence as close to the tree as possible and support the extensions next to it with short posts under the bottom rail. Set these short posts on concrete stepping stones.

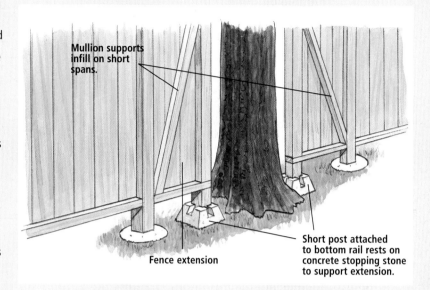

Mullion supports infill on short spans.

Fence extension

Short post attached to bottom rail rests on concrete stopping stone to support extension.

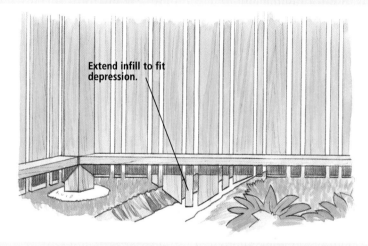

Extend infill to fit depression.

Shorten infill to fit obstruction.

Laying Out Sloped Fences

It would be nice if every fence site was perfectly level along its entire length, but few yards are perfectly flat. Fencing a slope requires some modification of the basic layout techniques shown earlier in this chapter. Essentially you have two options—contoured fencing or stepped fencing.

Contoured fencing is easier to install, especially on irregular or rolling slopes. The rails of a contoured frame run parallel to the slope and to each other, and the infill is cut to follow the slope. Rail fences and fences with surface-mounted infill make good contoured models. Inset infill does not work well with contoured fencing.

Stepped fencing resembles a stairway—its rails run horizontally and parallel to each other and each bay steps down the slope by an equal or unequal amount, depending on how you want the design to look. Stepped fences are more difficult to plan and install, so they are better suited to straight slopes. Almost any board fence can be adapted to a stepped fence.

Marking postholes on a slope requires a different technique than marking them on level ground. If you mark the width of the bays on the sloped ground, the posts will end up closer together than you want them. To space the posts correctly, you must mark them from a level line.

To establish a level line, drive a stake at each end of the slope where the end posts will be. Make the lower stake tall enough to be level with the top of the grade. Tie mason's line tightly between the stakes. On short slopes tie the upper end at grade level and slip a line level on it. On long slopes tie the line about a foot above grade so you'll have room to use a water level to level the line at the lower stake. Tape the line at intervals equal to your bay width and drop a plumb bob at the tapes to mark the postholes.

ESTABLISHING A LEVEL LINE

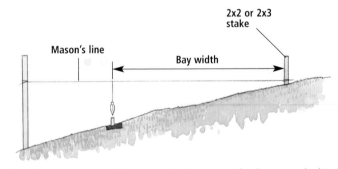

▲ Sloped fencing starts by staking out a level line across the slope. Tape the line at intervals equal to the width of the bays and mark posthole locations by dropping a plumb bob at the tapes.

STAKING A CONTOURED LAYOUT

▲ To stake out a contoured fence, establish a level line and mark your posthole locations. Then take down the stakes from the level line and drive batterboards at both the top and bottom of the slope and at every change in grade. Tie mason's line between them. Adjust the position of the line until it lies in the same plane along its length. Adjust the posthole markers to fall directly under the mason's line.

TYPICAL CONTOURED FRAMEWORK

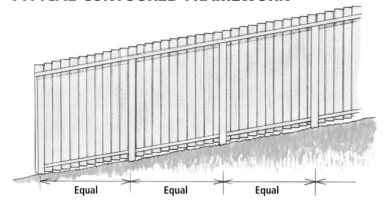

◀ Both contoured and stepped fences require that you mark the bay width (the posthole locations) using a level line. Otherwise your posts will be spaced incorrectly.

Equal   Equal   Equal

TYPICAL STEPPED FRAMEWORK

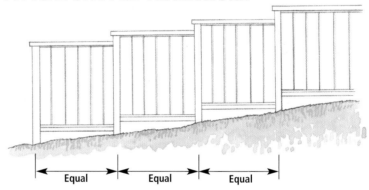

Equal   Equal   Equal

STAKING A STEPPED LAYOUT

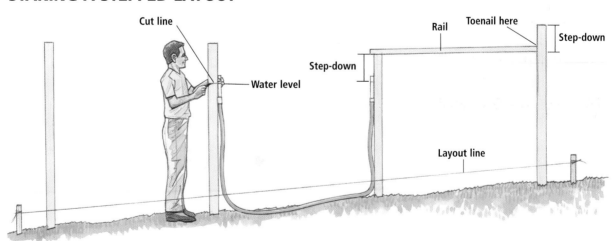

Cut line

Water level

Rail

Toenail here

Step-down

Step-down

Layout line

1 To stake out a stepped fence, establish a level line and post locations using the techniques described opposite. Set each post in concrete, leaving them taller than their final length. Let the concrete cure.

2 Measure the exact rise and run of the slope and compute the step-down distance.

3 Mark the step-down—measuring from the top—on the uppermost post. With a water level, mark the next post down at that height. Cut that post to height, mark the step-down on it, and repeat for the next post. Repeat for all of the posts.

BUILDING AN EDGE-RAIL FENCE FRAME

Almost all fence designs rely on one of two rail styles—edge rails or flat rails. Edge rails are installed with the widest of their faces perpendicular to the ground. That means they resist sagging more effectively than flat rails. This positioning also allows you more choices when it comes to mounting the infill (although most kinds of inset infill require flat rails, not edge rails).

Where you position the rails is largely a matter of design choice, but the rail position will affect the kind of infill and the method you use for hanging it. Some designs will call for the rails to be set flush with the posts along the entire length of the fence. Others will require flush rails that alternate from one side of the posts to the other on every other bay. Other designs will look better with the rails mounted on the surface of the posts, centered between them, or mounted in notches.

One of the primary decisions you'll need to make is which side of the fence will be the neighbor's—and whether it matters. Certain fence designs are clearly one-sided. Even though the fence you're building is *your* fence and it's on *your* property or property line, legal ownership will not necessarily prevent hard feelings if the neighbors have to look at the "back" side of it.

Always measure the rail locations from the top of the posts, not the bottom.

Usually 6"

Scatter the 2x4 rails around the fence line to keep them close at hand for assembly.

Bottom rail 3" to 6" above the ground

1 Lay out the fence line and set the posts in concrete. Let the concrete cure and leave the braces up—they add stability when you're driving fasteners. Cut the posts to the correct height and measure down from the top of each post to mark the location of the top and bottom rails. For fences on level ground, you can mark the end posts and snap a chalk line to mark the intermediate posts. For stepped or contoured frames, you'll have to measure and mark each pair of posts separately. Distribute the rails around the fence line so they will be handy.

2 Mark each rail for cutting, either by measuring the distance between posts or by holding the uncut rail in place and marking it, as shown here. Don't cut all the rails at once—the space between each pair of posts may vary a fraction of an inch, and rails that are even ⅛ inch short won't reach. Always saw just to the outside of your mark to make your rail fit snugly.

Support one end of the rail with scrap wood.

Such neighborly disagreements can be acrimonious but can often be avoided by constructing any number of "friendly" fences—designs that look good from both sides.

It can also help to give the neighbors some warning that you're going to build a fence. Showing them a friendly design will allay some of their fears and indicate to them that you respect their feelings. After all, the fence might be yours, but the view is community property.

Whatever the position of the rails, use the techniques illustrated to install them.

3 Predrill the holes for fasteners and toenail the top rails to the posts with 10d nails, 3½-inch galvanized or treated screws, or rail hangers. Then attach the bottom rails. When the frame is complete, remove the braces if you have not done so already.

LINE UP CENTERED RAILS

If your rails will be centered inside the post faces, mark the center of the posts and the rails after you cut them. When you attach the rails, line the marks up with each other.

SURFACE RAILS

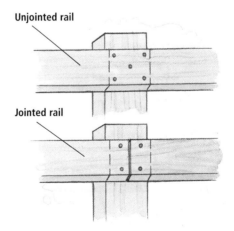

Unjointed rail

Jointed rail

If your edge-mounted rails will be fastened to the outside faces of the posts, use one of the nailing patterns above, depending on whether the rails are jointed or unjointed.

BUILDING A FLAT-RAIL FRAME

Flat-rail designs are suited to both surface-mounted and inset infill. In both cases the rails are fastened with their narrow edges flush with the faces of the posts. For surface-mounted infill, this provides a surface on which to fasten the boards between the frames. For inset infill, the wide faces of the rails provide plenty of space to attach both infill and the stops or nailers that hold them in place.

Although building a flat-rail frame involves essentially the same techniques as building edge-rail framing, a few details need additional attention:

■ First, because one of the functions of the top rail is to tie the posts together in a single structural unit, and because joints reduce the top rail's strength, you should minimize the number of joints. When you shop for rail stock, get the longest boards possible—on short fences, preferably a board that will span the entire length of the fence. In any case use top-rail stock long enough to span at least three posts.

■ Second, always butt top rails on the center of a post. This adds strength to the joint and gives you a surface wide enough for your fasteners. The same goes for cap-rail stock. If you're installing a cap rail, you can attach it at any time in the process of building the frame (but after fastening the top rail, of course).

Although flat rails are by nature more prone to sag than edge rails, there are a couple of things you can do to shore them up. A kickboard mounted under the bottom of the lower rail and toenailed at both ends to the posts will add a surprising amount of strength to the bay, and it

Distribute the rails around the fence line so they will be handy.

1 Lay out the fence line and set the posts in concrete. Let the concrete cure and leave the braces up—they add stability. Cut the posts to the correct height and measure down from the top of each post to mark the location of the bottom rails. For fences on level ground, you can mark the end posts and snap a chalk line to mark the intermediate posts. For stepped or contoured frames, you'll have to measure and mark each pair of posts separately.

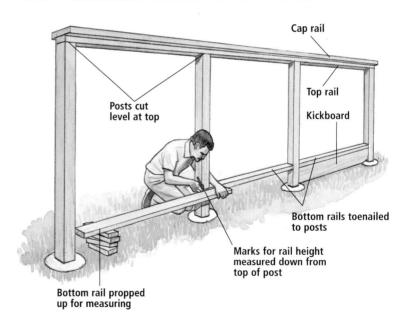

Cap rail

Posts cut level at top

Top rail

Kickboard

Bottom rails toenailed to posts

Marks for rail height measured down from top of post

Bottom rail propped up for measuring

2 Use the longest top-rail stock possible to reduce the number of joints. Cut the top-rail sections so any joints will be centered on the top of the posts. Predrill the top-rail sections and fasten them to the posts with 10d nails or 3½-inch galvanized or treated screws. Then measure, cut, and attach the cap rail, bottom rails, and kickboards.

will help keep the whole assembly from sagging under its own weight. So will one or two additional rails within the bay–mounted either horizontally or vertically, depending on your design.

Because you might find it difficult to set a kickboard in the space between the bottom rail and the ground after the rail is fastened, screw the kickboard to the bottom of the rail first and then toenail the assembled pieces between the posts.

Like edge rails, you can set flat rails at various heights from the ground and in dadoes cut in the interior faces of the posts. Varying the height of dadoed rails from bay to bay can make the "back" side of the fence more attractive.

FASTENING THE TOP RAIL

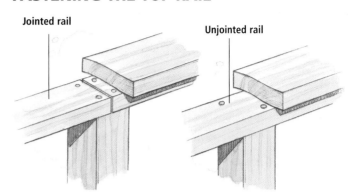

Jointed rail

Unjointed rail

How you drive the top-rail fasteners will depend on whether the rail is unjointed or jointed. Use the pattern above that is appropriate to your installation. Fasten the cap rail with the same patterns, but do not install a cap-rail joint over a top-rail joint. Offset cap-rail joints by at least one post.

INSTALLING A KICKBOARD

Kickboards close the gap under the bottom rail, add a decorative touch to your fence, and keep animals from crawling under it. They also help keep flat rails from sagging. You can attach them to the surface of the posts or inset them under the bottom rail. It's usually easier to install an inset kickboard on the bottom rail and toenail the entire assembly to the posts. Fasten the kickboard to the bottom of the rail with 3-inch screws every 8 to 10 inches. Toenail it to the posts at the ends. Trim your kickboard with a 1×2 if you want. Make the kickboard from pressure-treated lumber or the heartwood of a decay-resistant species such as cedar or cypress because the board touches the earth and is subject to rot.

Surface-mounted kickboard

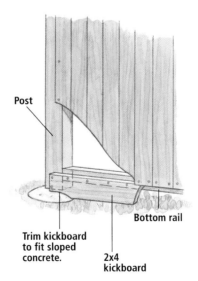

Post

Trim kickboard to fit sloped concrete.

2x4 kickboard

Bottom rail

Inset kickboard

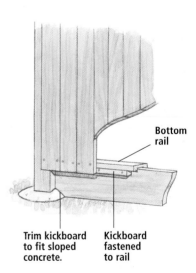

Bottom rail

Trim kickboard to fit sloped concrete.

Kickboard fastened to rail

Cutting Notches, Mortises, and Tenons

Notches, tenons, and mortises increase the strength of fencing joints and enhance the aesthetic appeal of a fence design. If you haven't cut them before, you'll find the skill easy to acquire (take a few practice cuts on scrap). Make sure your cutting tools are sharp. Sharp tools are safer than dull tools and produce better looking–and better fitting–joints.

Although it's possible to cut these joints after setting the posts, it's a lot easier to cut them all at once before putting the posts into the postholes. This means that the joints must be at the same height from post to post or your fence will look crooked. Mark the position of the cuts precisely so they're the same from post to post, always measuring down from the top of the post to the joint. Then use the method illustrated on page 31 to bring the posts level with each other when setting them.

NOTCHING POSTS

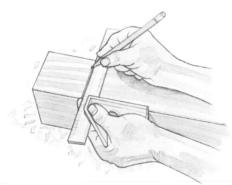

1 Using the width of your rails as the measurement, mark the top and bottom of the notch on the post with a combination square or layout square.

2 Set your circular saw to the depth of the notch (the thickness of the rail stock, commonly ¾ inch). Line up the side of the saw with the cut line and cut a series of kerfs about ¼ inch apart.

3 Break the kerfed waste from the notch with a hammer, taking care to not mar the edge of the notch.

4 Remove the waste with a wide, sharp chisel (bevel side down), clearing away the ridges until the bottom face of the notch is smooth and flat.

CUTTING MORTISE AND TENON JOINTS

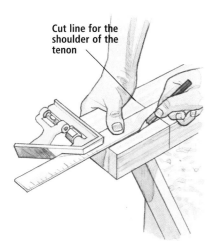

Cut line for the shoulder of the tenon

1 Mark the tenon's length (for a blind mortise, about 1/16 inch shorter than the depth of the mortise) on all four sides of the stock, using a combination or layout square. In a through mortise, the tenon should be 1/8 inch longer than the thickness of the mortised stock.

2 Clamp the tenon stock in a bench vise and, using a backsaw, carefully cut through the end of the stock to the shoulder line on all four sides. When you reach the shoulder line, make sure you saw perpendicular to the wood.

3 Clamp the tenon stock in a miter box and, using a backsaw, cut on the shoulder line to remove the waste. Repeat on the remaining sides.

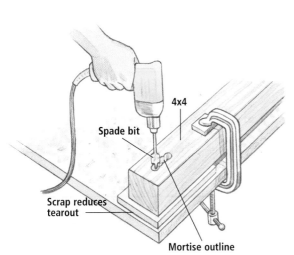

4x4

Spade bit

Scrap reduces tearout

Mortise outline

Chisel

4 Mortises, like notches, must be cut on the same plane on each post. Measure down from the top of each post so all the mortises begin at the same height. Then, using scrap or a cardboard template cut to the same size as the finished tenon, mark the outline of the mortise on the surface of the post. Using a spade bit about the same diameter as the width of the mortise, drill overlapping holes to remove most of the waste.

5 After drilling, clean up the sides of the mortise with a sharp chisel. Tap gently with a mallet. Gently smooth the surface with the flat side of the chisel. Be particular about the mortise corners; they must be smooth and square. For a through mortise, turn the workpiece over and use the chisel to clean up the other side too.

INSTALLING SURFACE-MOUNTED INFILL

O f all the aspects of fence construction, installing the infill is probably the most enjoyable. That's because from here on out your work is "downhill," and you can begin to see the results of your planning and layout. It's at this step that the structure you've been toiling over begins to look like a fence. Besides, the tasks associated with hanging the infill are generally repetitive—you'll fall into a rhythm, and the work will go quickly.

Surface-mounted infill requires less measuring and fitting than inset infill, so fences built this way go up quickly. You don't even need to precut boards to length for surface-mounted infill when fencing on level ground; you can let the boards run wild—at random heights—and then cut them to a finished line all at once. Infill boards finished with a cut top—pickets, points, or dog ears, for example—must be cut to size before you put them up.

One of the trickiest jobs is to get the bottom of each board lined up with the adjacent one. Tack a batten along the bottom of the posts—spanning at least three posts—and this task becomes a snap. The batten allows you to set each infill board directly on it—it's like having a third hand. Level the batten if the ground is level; let it follow the slope for a contoured fence. Whether level or sloped, keep the batten at the same distance from the ground along its length by measuring and marking its location from the top of the posts. Don't try to "eyeball" the clearance between the ground and the batten—it's almost impossible to get it right without measuring.

■ If your fasteners are less than 2 inches from the ends of the infill boards, predrill holes to keep the infill from splitting. Fasteners 2 inches or more from the ends of the infill are less likely to split the wood, but it's still wise to drill pilot holes.

■ If the infill goes out of plumb, remove it and correct the problem—it's easier in the long run to fix a mistake early than to try adjusting subsequent boards.

■ Mark the height of your infill on both ends of the bay, snap a chalk line between the marks, and trim the infill along the line. To cut it quickly and accurately with a circular saw, measure down from the chalk line a distance equal to the distance from your circular saw's blade to the edge of its soleplate. Watch out for uneven joints; they will catch the saw.

■ If you are staining or painting the fence and didn't do so before installation, prepare the surfaces according to the finish manufacturer's instructions and apply the finish. Protect your landscaping and plantings with plastic tarps.

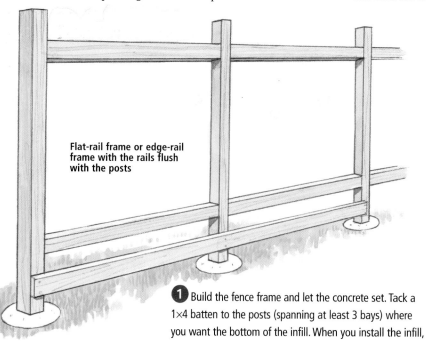

Flat-rail frame or edge-rail frame with the rails flush with the posts

1 Build the fence frame and let the concrete set. Tack a 1×4 batten to the posts (spanning at least 3 bays) where you want the bottom of the infill. When you install the infill, set each board on the batten. This will keep the infill at a consistent height above the ground.

2 Distribute your infill materials along the fence line so they're close at hand. Begin fastening the infill at an end, corner, or gate post. Attach 1× stock with 8d nails or 2-inch treated screws; hang thinner material with 6d nails or 1½-inch screws. Check the leading edge of the infill with a carpenter's level every 3 or 4 feet to make sure it is plumb.

Let top edge of infill run wild.

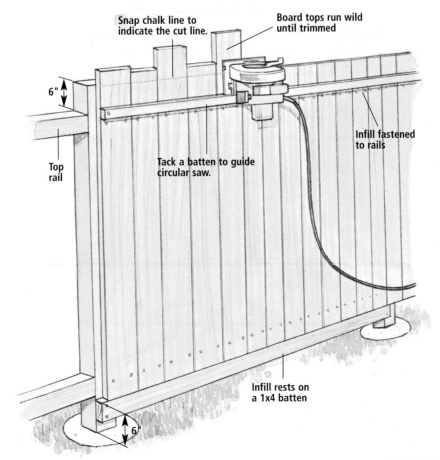

Snap chalk line to indicate the cut line.

Board tops run wild until trimmed

6"

Top rail

Tack a batten to guide circular saw.

Infill fastened to rails

Infill rests on a 1x4 batten

6"

3 Mark the finished height of the completed infill at both ends of the fence, tack a guide to the fence, and trim the infill with a circular saw.

INSTALLING INSET INFILL

nset infill lends itself to a host of fence styles–it's the ideal way to install lattice panels as well as other types of panel fencing–plywood, acrylic, and tongue-and-groove. You'll also use it if you're building a basket weave or featherboard fence. With its 1× or 2× stops containing the infill boards and functioning as trim, it creates a stylish finished look for a variety of materials.

Inset infill requires careful marking of the position of the stops and more exacting construction, but it produces clean lines and shows an equally attractive face on both sides. It's the ideal construction if you're looking for a friendly fence that will appeal to your next-door neighbors.

Your planning should include careful computation of the total width of the infill boards and stops. Because a 2×4 rail is actually 3½ inches wide, you'll have to make sure of two things:
■ That the combined width of the materials does not exceed the width of the rails.
■ That the entire assembly, infill boards and stops together, is centered in the frame.

Add the width of the pieces together and subtract it from the width of the rails. Divide the remaining amount in half: This is the width of the "reveal," the space between the edge of the stop and the edge of the rail. Thus the combined width of 1× infill and 1× stops–2¼ inches–leaves 1¼ inches of rail exposed. Set your first stop ⅝ inch from the edge of the rails (1¼/2=⅝ inch). Use a combination square set to ⅝ inch to mark each interior corner of the frame. Snap chalk lines at these marks and nail the stops on the lines. Inset infill requires square fence frames, but you can usually work around minor flaws. Wide stops, for example, can hide gaps. And you can cut sheet materials to fit exactly.

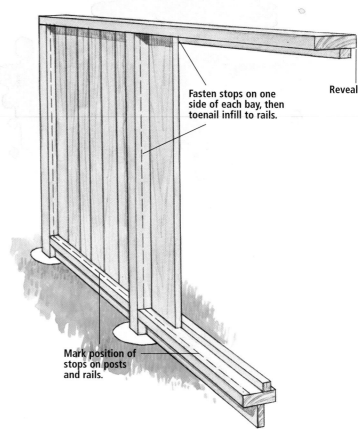

Reveal

Fasten stops on one side of each bay, then toenail infill to rails.

Mark position of stops on posts and rails.

1 Mark the position of the stops and snap guide lines on the posts and rails. Cut the stops and infill to length. Fasten the stops to one side of the bay opening with either 6d or 8d finishing nails, depending on the thickness of the stops. Working from the open side, fit the infill into the frame. Toenail the infill to the rails, not to the stops. Check for plumb as you go.

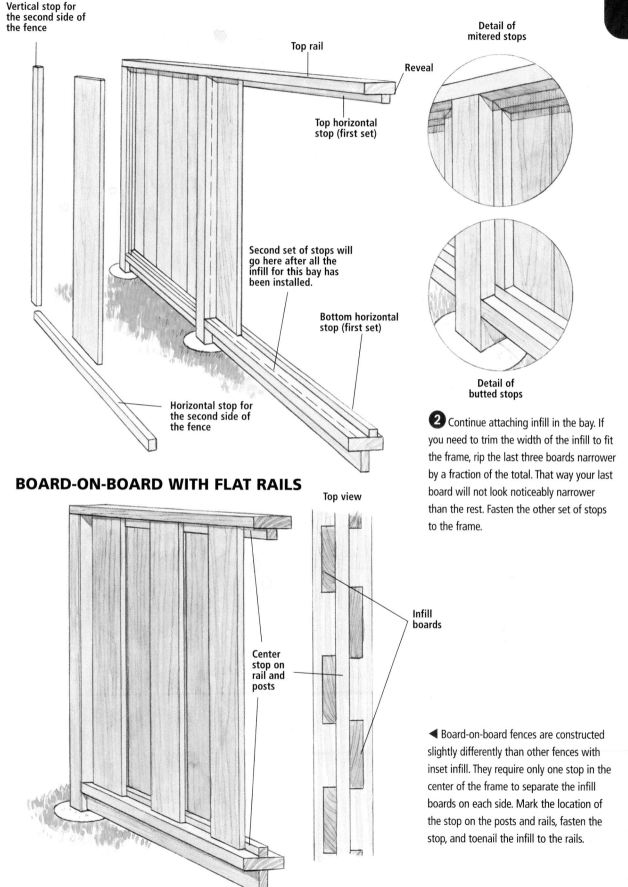

Vertical stop for the second side of the fence

Top rail

Reveal

Top horizontal stop (first set)

Detail of mitered stops

Second set of stops will go here after all the infill for this bay has been installed.

Bottom horizontal stop (first set)

Horizontal stop for the second side of the fence

Detail of butted stops

2 Continue attaching infill in the bay. If you need to trim the width of the infill to fit the frame, rip the last three boards narrower by a fraction of the total. That way your last board will not look noticeably narrower than the rest. Fasten the other set of stops to the frame.

BOARD-ON-BOARD WITH FLAT RAILS

Top view

Center stop on rail and posts

Infill boards

◀ Board-on-board fences are constructed slightly differently than other fences with inset infill. They require only one stop in the center of the frame to separate the infill boards on each side. Mark the location of the stop on the posts and rails, fasten the stop, and toenail the infill to the rails.

HANDY INFILL INSTALLATION TIPS

No matter what kind of fence you're building, following a few general tips will make it better looking, professionally built, and longer lasting.

■ Don't scrimp on fasteners—either in quality or quantity. Treated nails or deck screws cost slightly more but will last longer and stain the fence less than untreated fasteners. Galvanized fasteners are not immune from rust. Stainless-steel fasteners are the best choice.

■ In addition to their own weight, fences have to carry the loads imposed by rain, snow, wind, and climbing kids. Much of this stress falls on the fasteners—use plenty of them.

■ Hang boards plumb. Check the infill as you go—every few feet at least—with a 4-foot level (shorter levels won't be accurate). If the infill has gotten out of plumb, take your work apart and correct it. Out-of-plumb infill only gets worse.

■ Make bottom edges flush and smooth. Use battens to help place the infill (tack a 1×3 or 1×4 to the surface of the posts) unless your design intentionally calls for random lengths. Reposition the batten as you work your way down the line.

■ To finish a wild-top edge, chalk a line at the cutting height. Then tack a 1×3 or 1×4 guide so a circular saw's soleplate can ride on it. Set the blade deep enough to cut through the infill, but no deeper. Rest the saw on the cutting guide and cut the entire top of the fence in one pass.

SPACING THE INFILL

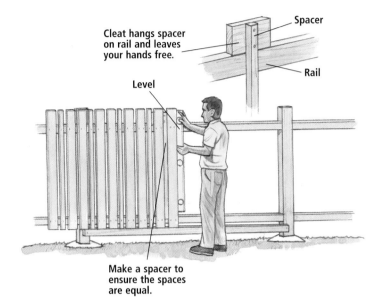

Cleat hangs spacer on rail and leaves your hands free.

Spacer

Rail

Level

Make a spacer to ensure the spaces are equal.

▲ Equalize the spaces between infill boards with a cleated spacer. Hang the cleat on the top rail so you can free both hands to hold the infill as you fasten it. Check the infill for plumb every 3 or 4 feet.

CUTTING ANGLED INFILL

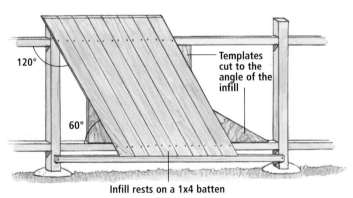

120°

60°

Templates cut to the angle of the infill

Infill rests on a 1x4 batten

▲ Cut templates to properly position angled infill in the frame. Cut the bottom of the infill to the correct angle and set the boards on a level batten while you fasten them. Cut the top edge to length or let the tops of the boards run wild and trim them with a circular saw. Use another batten to guide the saw and keep the top edge straight.

BUILDING CURVED FENCE SECTIONS

Building a curved fence section requires a careful layout (see page 128). Once you have the arc scribed on the ground, use the directions illustrated to locate and set the posts and install the rails–either curved or segmented. Hang the infill as you would on a straight rail.

You should construct your curved fence section in the same manner as the straight sections. For example, if you built the straight sections with flush-mounted rails, your curved section will have to follow suit. The best solution is to design the fence so the rails are notched into the posts. If your straight rails are face-mounted, your curved rails should be too.

1 For segmented rails, start by determining the angle for the rail ends. Tack a level 2×4 to the outside edges of two posts. Hold a straightedge against the side face of one post and extend the line across the top of the 2×4. Cut the 2×4 at this angle and use it as a template to cut all the rails.

2 Cut the rails to fit between the posts for flush-mounted rails, as shown in the upper illustration. Install surface-mounted rails as shown in the lower illustration.

SEGMENTED RAILS

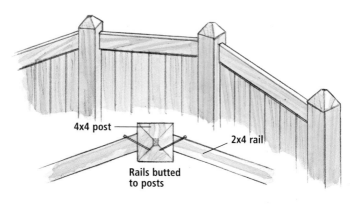

4x4 post — Rails butted to posts — 2x4 rail

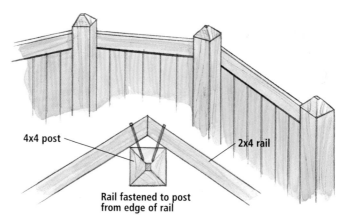

4x4 post — Rail fastened to post from edge of rail — 2x4 rail

CONTINUOUS CURVE

1 Make the rails from layers of thin stock—four layers of ⅜-inch redwood, two layers of 1×4 redwood with ¼-inch saw kerfs spaced 1½ to 2 inches apart, or unkerfed 1×4 redwood for shallow bends. Soak the rails in water to make them more pliable.

2 Fasten the first rail layer on the posts (or into 3½×1½-inch notches) with 2-inch screws. Butt-join successive pieces at the center of a post. Cut the next layer so the joint won't fall on top of a joint in the first layer. Fasten this layer with screws long enough to go through both layers and into the post.

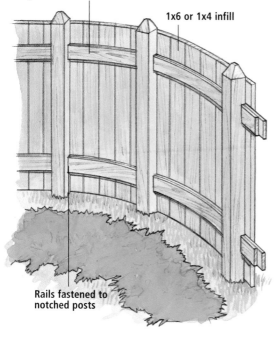

Two layers of 1x4 redwood for rails

1x6 or 1x4 infill

Rails fastened to notched posts

FINISHING
OUTDOOR PROJECTS

O utdoor projects must withstand a lot of abuse from the elements, and that requires some preplanning and possibly a durable finish.

Redwood, cedar, or pressure-treated wood left unfinished will soon take on a weathered look, complete with natural checks and slight surface imperfections. Depending on the species, these woods will eventually turn some shade of gray–a color that does not indicate deterioration, but one you may not find appealing. If you prefer the rich, natural hue of brand new lumber, apply a product that protects the surface of the wood and helps it stand up to harsh outdoor conditions.

Wood left outdoors has two formidable foes: moisture and the ultraviolet (UV) rays of sunlight. Different exterior finishes provide different degrees of protection against them. Here's a survey of your choices:

Clear finishes for natural colors
Spar varnish, polyurethane varnish, water repellents, and penetrating oils shield wood from water while allowing all the color to show through. But clear finishes let UV rays penetrate into the grain. The wood cells react with these rays and begin to deteriorate under the film. The wood darkens, and the finish cracks, blisters, and peels.

Adding a UV filtering agent to the finish retards this reaction but doesn't eliminate it. If you use a clear finish, select one that has UV absorbers (the label will tell you). Even with UV protection, you'll have to reapply the finish at least every two years. If you wait until it peels, you'll face a tedious stripping job.

Stains
With light pigmentation, semitransparent stains let the wood's natural grain and texture show through. These stains are available in tones that closely match various woods. Brighter stains can either contrast with or complement your house, deck, or patio. Semitransparent stains come in both oil-base and water-base formulations that you'll have to recoat every year or two.

Semisolid stains have more pigment than semitransparent stains and offer more UV resistance as well. But they're not completely opaque. You can expect a semisolid stain to last about two years.

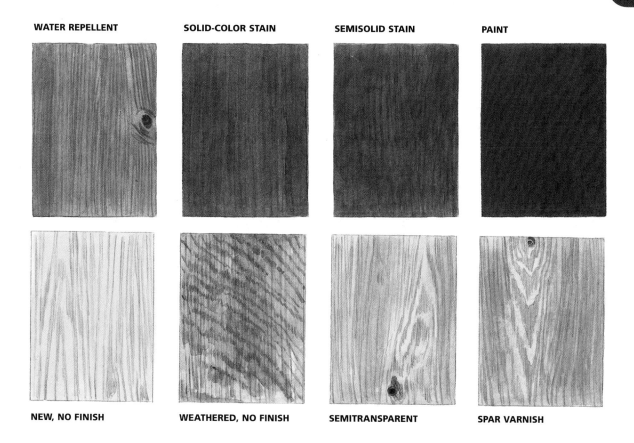

WATER REPELLENT   **SOLID-COLOR STAIN**   **SEMISOLID STAIN**   **PAINT**

NEW, NO FINISH   **WEATHERED, NO FINISH**   **SEMITRANSPARENT**   **SPAR VARNISH**

Opaque stains

Opaque stains, like paint, conceal the wood's natural color and grain pattern but allow some of the texture to show. They're available in a variety of natural-looking colors and brighter hues and with either an oil or latex base. You can choose either a flat opaque stain or a low-luster finish that's easier to wash.

Because the pigment in this type of stain is suspended in an oil or latex carrier, it's not designed to penetrate the pores of the wood. On horizontal surfaces especially, pigment that doesn't completely penetrate may collect, causing blotchy areas that wear off or blister. The California Redwood Association doesn't recommend using stains with a latex base on redwood products. Opaque stains usually need to be recoated every two years.

For treated lumber you may want to select a stain color compatible with the color imparted by the chemical treatment. Some chemicals will tinge the wood slightly, which can alter the effect of the stain.

Whatever stain or finish you use, experiment with different samples on scraps. Some manufacturers offer special 4-ounce samples that you can experiment with before selecting a particular product.

Paint

Paint is rarely used on the top grades of redwood or cedar because it hides grain, texture, and color. But it can be your solution to hiding the hue of treated wood, and it's the only way to protect metal parts.

If you decide to paint a wooden outdoor project—no matter what wood you've selected—be sure to apply an oil- or alkyd-base primer before applying the finish coat. For metal use a product that contains a rust inhibitor.

Horizontal surfaces will probably sustain much more wear than vertical surfaces (with the possible exception of handrails). Avoid the need for early renewal by selecting the highest-quality exterior-grade enamel available. And finally, while all these products retard or prevent deterioration, none of them succeeds completely (or for very long) without recoating. You'll need to repaint every two to three years.

Lighten up with bleach

Stains put color into wood. Bleaches take it out, letting you lighten almost any wood to nearly white. Use the right type of bleach for the job. Two-part bleach (sodium hydroxide and hydrogen peroxide) removes the natural color from wood. Chlorine bleach removes dye from wood, just as it removes color from

laundry. Oxalic acid removes rust and water stains. Whichever type you use, neutralize it afterward, following the manufacturer's instructions, sand lightly, then protect the wood with a clear finish.

Laying it on

After you've decided on a finish for a fence, you need to figure out how you're going to get it from the can onto the wood. The applicator that's right for this job depends partly on the finish you've chosen, partly on the amount of surface you have to cover, and partly on the look you want. Here are your options:

■ **Brushes:** These trusty tools get the nod for most finishing chores. Purchase brushes with synthetic bristles (nylon, polyester, or nylon/polyester blend) for water-base finishes and latex paints, and natural bristles (animal hair) for oil-base finishes and paints. The pores of natural bristles absorb water readily, making them puffy and hard to control with

Roller tray

Painting mitten

Standard roller

Pad painter

Foam brushes

Trim roller

Synthetic-bristle brush

Corner pad painter

Natural-bristle brush

Pressure
spray gun

water-base finishes. Oil-base finishes will attack and break down synthetic bristles, so you'll end up with bristles sticking to the surface. Disposable foam brushes work fine with either type of finish and do an especially good job with stains. Their biggest drawback is that they don't last long. Even for a medium-size fence, you might be better off buying a bristled brush instead.

■ **Rollers:** Rollers make short work of large, flat surfaces, and you can buy smaller trim rollers for tight spots. Both types have a plastic or wood handle (often threaded to accept an extension pole) and a metal frame that holds the napped cover.

The type of finish (water or oil base) determines the type of roller cover to use. Most covers are made from mohair, lamb's wool, acetate, or polyurethane foam and are labeled for which finish they are appropriate.

Roller covers vary in nap depths from $\frac{1}{16}$ inch to $1\frac{1}{2}$ inches. Use a long-nap roller for rough surfaces, a short-nap one for smooth work. The nap, in turn, is fastened to a cardboard or plastic sleeve. If you use a water-base finish, buy a roller with a plastic sleeve. For an oil-base finish, get one with a cardboard sleeve.

■ **Pads and mittens:** Pad painters have a carpetlike material or plastic foam inserted in a plastic, moplike applicator or a paintbrush handle. Though excellent for applying paint to almost any surface, they work especially well on irregular surfaces such as shakes, fencing, screening, and lattice.

A painting mitten makes coating railings, spindles, and similar items easy. You need only put on a thin, disposable plastic glove to keep your hand clean, then put on the thick-nap mitten and dip the mitten into the finish. You can quickly coat a railing or spindle by

grasping it and sliding the mitten along its length. And you can poke finish into narrow or cramped places where a brush would spatter.

■ **Sprayers:** For a smooth, rich finish that goes on quickly, consider spraying your project with an aerosol spray can or an air-operated spray gun. Spraying can be messy, of course, but some aerosol sprays shoot finish through a pad like the one on a pad painter.

Pressurized equipment has become neater too, thanks to high-volume, low-pressure (HVLP) equipment, which wastes less finish and reduces overspray. Conventional spray guns blast out air at up to 40 pounds per square inch (psi). HVLP units need 4 to 10 psi to get the job done; up to 85 percent of the finish lands on the workpiece instead of 36 percent with conventional sprayers. (The percentage that doesn't go onto the project goes into the air as overspray and settles on everything in the vicinity.)

▶ **Because wood edges can nick and splinter, it's a good idea to round them off with a light sanding. Hold the sanding block at an angle; use gentle pressure and a rocking motion. A molded rubber sanding block like the one shown lets you control the angle so it's consistent along the length of the board.**

CHAPTER HIGHLIGHTS

Fences and gates are subjected to

harsh weather conditions and the

stresses of use. This chapter illustrates

techniques you can use to make major

and minor repairs to your fences

and gates.

REPAIRING FENCES AND GATES

Because maintenance is less expensive than repair, it can pay to conduct a regular inspection of your fences. Fences are not like decks—we don't use them every day, and generally they are more removed from centers of outdoor activity. That means aspects that need repair go unnoticed. Put "inspect fences" on your calendar— at least once every year.

Use a screwdriver to poke around the base of posts set in concrete to check for rot. For earth-and-gravel backfill, dig down about 6 inches. Soft or spongy wood means rot

has set in. Replace the post—it will gradually weaken the fence. Look for rot where the rails meet the infill or posts.

If the posts aren't plumb, nature will loosen the rails until the fence comes apart. Realign and reset the posts and refasten the rails and the infill.

Fences look better and wear longer when the finish repels moisture. If your fence is painted or stained, a re-coat can add years to its life.

Add years of service to your fences and gates by using the easy techniques in this chapter.

MAKING RAIL REPAIRS

Rails seldom deteriorate along the middle of a fence bay. Any damage they sustain usually occurs at one end of the rail or the other. That's where rot begins–more often on the bottom rail than on the top, because moisture collects on the fence and runs down and evaporates up from the soil. The bottom rail also tends to be more "sheltered" and is not able to dry out as quickly as the top rail.

One of the first signs of rail damage is loose fasteners. Before you rip off the rail, try resetting loose nails. At best this will probably turn out to be a temporary fix because by the time you realize the fasteners are loose, the stress on the joint has probably enlarged the hole and removed enough wood fibers that the nail is left with nothing to grip.

If the rail works loose again after a couple of days, try removing the nails and refastening the rail with #10×4-inch coated screws (or screws that will be long enough to reach into fresh wood without going through the other side). As a last resort, you can support the rail with several braces. These braces also are likely to be temporary–if a new fastener won't hold the rail in place, it's a pretty good bet that the rail harbors some other form of structural problem and needs replacing. Bracing, however, will buy you some time, even though you may not consider it the most aesthetically appealing solution.

Removing and replacing a rail will cost you some time, but not a great expenditure of energy. The most time-consuming aspect of this job is getting all the fasteners out. If the infill is

▲ To tighten loose nails, reset them with a nail set. If the rail is still loose, remove the nails and drive in longer nails or treated screws.

fastened with nails, don't try to pry them out without first prying away the infill from the back side of the fence. Then go around to the front side of the fence and tap each infill board back on the rail. The board should move but the nail should not, leaving its head exposed. When you pry out the nails, slip a piece of 1× scrap under the hammer head–it will increase your leverage and keep the wood from denting. Before you remove the rail, mark its location so you know where to put the new one.

Removing the rail does not require much finesse, because it's damaged anyway. Don't try to pry it out–you may tear up the post. If it's screwed in place, remove the screws. If it's nailed, give one end a couple of solid blows with your hammer (or small sledge), and it should fall away with the nails intact. Pull the rail from the other end with a twist.

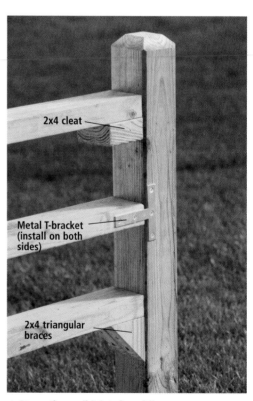

2x4 cleat

Metal T-bracket (install on both sides)

2x4 triangular braces

▲ Strengthen rail joints by adding a 2x4 cleat, metal T-bracket ,or triangular bracing.

REPLACING A RAIL

1 To replace a rail, first mark its location on the posts so you can install its replacement in the same place. Then remove the fasteners that attach the infill. To remove nails, work from the back side of the fence and pry the infill away from the rail with a pry bar. Then work from the front side of the fence and drive the infill back against the rail, exposing the nail head. Remove the nails with a pry bar. To remove screws, use a cordless drill. Once you have the infill fasteners out, remove the rail from the posts.

Remove fasteners on damaged rail only.

2 Repair fastener holes in the posts as necessary (see pages 162–163). Then, to help you position the new rail, clamp a piece of 2×4 scrap on both posts at the location of the old rail.

3 Measure the distance between posts (don't measure the old rail; it may have shrunk), and cut a new rail to this length. Set the rail on the 2×4 blocks and toenail it to the posts. Then go back to the front side of the fence and install new infill fasteners, keeping the infill plumb as you go.

ADDING POSTS

A sagging fence bay may be an indication that gravity has gradually taken its toll, and the weight of the infill is more than the rails can support and remain level. This a problem you might be able to remedy by jacking up the center of the bay with a pneumatic jack (just under the edge of the bottom rail) and installing a 2× kickboard. However, a sagging bay may also be an indication of serious post damage. If damaged posts are the problem and replacing the entire fence is not feasible, you can add a post in the center of the affected bay(s).

Mark the center of the bay and locate the new posthole. You can't get a clamshell digger centered on the hole because the fence is in the way, but you can come close, digging most of the hole with the digger and enlarging it from the other side with a round-nosed shovel. Once you've dug the hole, you can set the post in it and mark the post for the location of the notches.

It's not critical at this step that the notches in the post are at exactly the precise height. What is critical is that their spacing is the same as the rail spacing and that the notches in the rails are plumb with each other (which will keep the post plumb when you set it).

What kind of notch you cut will depend on whether the rails are set flat or on edge (see illustrations, below). You can notch the post with a circular saw, cutting kerfs and chiseling out the waste as shown on page 136. The circular saw will also work when notching the rail, but the weight of the saw might make it difficult to work with when holding it upright. Using a jigsaw (and the same kerfing technique) will make this cut easier. Just make sure you cut the kerfs to the same depth.

When you set the notched post in the ground, tap it into the notches and tack it to the rails from the back of the post. You can level the rails with your method of choice. A pneumatic jack is shown, but most screw jacks made for changing tires on today's automobiles will work also.

If you don't have a suitable jack, have a helper level the bay with a tamping bar levered on wood blocks. Keep the bay level with another set of blocks while you backfill the hole. Whatever device you use to level the bay, leave it in place until the concrete cures. When the concrete has set, strengthen the notches with additional fasteners.

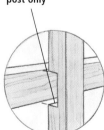
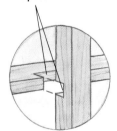

Flat rail: notch both rail and post

Edge rail: notch post only

1 To add a new post to a sagging bay, mark the center of the top rail and drop a plumb bob from the mark to locate the new posthole.

2 Dig the new posthole and shovel in about 4 inches of gravel. Set the new post in the hole and hold it plumb against the rails. Mark the position of the notches on the post and cut both the post and rail notches. Set the post back in the hole and fasten the rails into the notches, keeping the post plumb. At this point the bay will still sag—you'll adjust it in the next step.

Cut new post to same height as existing posts.

3 Set a carpenter's level on the bottom rail and level the rail with a pneumatic jack. When the rail is level, shovel and tamp concrete in the posthole. Leave the jack in place until the concrete sets. Then use a level line to mark the new post at the height of the existing posts and cut the new post to the same height.

REPLACING POSTS

If a post is rotted below ground and the above ground section is sound, you can replace it with a new one or shore it up as shown on page 156.

Although shoring up a post is a repair that can last a long time, the repair will be obvious, and you may find its appearance distracting. In this case, replacing the post is the way to go. It essentially returns the fence to its original form. In any case, if the visible section of the post is damaged, you should replace it.

A post replacement requires stripping the infill from the bays on either side of the post and removing the rails. Because you'll want to reuse all this lumber, exercise some care when taking the bays apart. Slip a short length of scrap wood under your hammer or pry bar (or cat's paw) when prying up nails. The scrap will give you a little more leverage and protect the surface of the wood. Loosen the infill from the back side of the fence, opposite, before pulling nails. If the fence is assembled with screws, make sure you remove all of them before taking a board down. Any screws that were overdriven when the fence was built may look like empty holes. When you try to remove a board that's still partly fastened, you'll rip the wood.

Pulling posts from the ground can be difficult work. In almost every case, you'll have to dig to at least ⅔ of the depth of the post and usually to the bottom—at least on one side of it. No matter how much soil you remove, work the post back and forth before pulling it out. If the post breaks at the rotted section, you may have to dig it out in pieces, using a tamping bar to break it apart.

Scrap increases leverage

Dig soil out around post base or concrete footing.

① To replace a post, remove the infill from the bays on both sides of the post, then remove the rails. Add a piece of scrap under your pry bar to increase your leverage when pulling nails and to minimize damage to the rail.

② Dig out the soil around the post or around the concrete footing—as wide and deep as you can. The more soil you remove, the easier it will be to remove the post. Then work the post back and forth to loosen it from the soil. Pull the post free if possible. If you can't, pull it up as shown in the next step.

3 Loose posts will come free from the soil if you apply the proper leverage. Some can be pried out by driving a wrecking bar into the base of the post and pushing down on the bar supported by a block of wood on the ground. Stubborn posts may require the bar-and-chain device shown here. Fasten the chain tightly around the post and a tamping bar. Then insert a piece of railroad tie or other large "fulcrum" and push down on the bar to lift the post. If the post still won't come free, dig out more soil around it.

Tamping bar

Railroad tie or other fulcrum

Utility chain with hook

Tack mason's lines to keep the new post in line.

4 To make sure your new post is lined up with the existing posts, tack mason's line to the faces of the old posts at both the top and bottom of the fence. Shovel 4 inches of gravel into the hole if necessary and set the new post in place. Brace the post plumb in both directions, making sure it just touches the mason's lines. Shovel in concrete and let it cure. Then tack a tight line to the tops of the existing posts and cut the new post to the same height. Replace the rails and infill.

SHORING UP A DAMAGED POST

Shoring up a damaged post can result in a permanent repair if done correctly. It requires that most of the above ground surface of the post be damage-free. Before you start this job, support the post with blocks. That way you won't damage fasteners or the rest of the frame when you cut away the damaged section.

The most difficult part of this job may be removing any concrete around the post. Not too long ago, traditional post-setting methods called only for a concrete collar to keep water out. Removing a collar will take a bit of time, but most will come away if you crack them with a cold chisel. You may even be able to crack the collar with a sharp blow from a small sledge. A hammer drill equipped with a cold chisel will also do the job. Wear eye protection when hammering or chiseling concrete.

If the post is set in a concrete footing, you won't be able to crack it. Dig out the footing instead (see page 154).

At some point in this process, you'll have to cut the post–when you do it is a matter of preference and the requirements of the job at hand. Whenever you cut the post, use a reciprocating saw and cut it a couple of inches above ground (and above the rotted section).

Enlarging the hole sufficiently to remove the bottom of a post may leave you with what looks like a crater under your fence. If the hole is obviously larger than the concrete needed for the new post (and will leave a large concrete circle in your yard), drop in a cardboard form tube and backfill the tube with soil. Then set the post in the form and tamp the concrete thoroughly when you pour it. You'll still need a layer of gravel with the tube form.

1 Brace the damaged post to keep the fence from sagging when you cut away the rotted section. Break up any concrete collar with a small sledge and cold chisel, remove it, and dig out around the post. If the post is set in a concrete footing, don't try to break it up; dig around the footing. Cut the post above the rotted section and remove it and any footing. Enlarge the hole to accommodate the new post section.

Stub post angled to shed water

2 Cut a new stub post, then shovel about 4 inches of gravel into the hole and set the stub post in. Plumb it and brace it as necessary (you may not need the braces on this short a post) or clamp it to the old post if it's plumb. Then fill the hole with tamped concrete. Let the concrete cure. You can drill the holes in the new post before you set it in the hole or after the concrete sets up.

Cut the new post from the same lumber as the original post. If you're in doubt, use pressure-treated stock rated for ground contact.

You can fasten the new post to the front of the old one as shown here or on the side of the old post. Attaching it to the side will allow you to clamp the two together, a step you might find makes plumbing the new post easier.

3 If you haven't done so already, drill holes for carriage bolts in the replacement post (but not in the old post). Check the rails with a carpenter's level to make sure they are level. Raise them with a pneumatic jack (see page 153) to level them, and leave the jack in place. Then use the holes in the replacement post as a guide to drill through the old post. Insert carriage bolts and tighten them, then remove the jack.

CHECKING FOR ROT

Moisture is the enemy of all wood, and when it takes up residence in a wooden structure, it shows up as rot.

Rot will often—but not always— display itself as a deep black coloring in the wood. If your wood is black, it's sure to be beyond repair (and unsafe if present in a load-bearing or structural member).

To check for rot, poke around the surface with a slot-tipped screwdriver. If the wood feels spongy and the screwdriver penetrates it without pressure, you'll need to replace the board.

STRAIGHTENING A LEANING FENCE

Even a well-constructed, perfectly set fence can develop a tendency to lean over time. Strong winds and heavy rains can work hard on a fence and cause it to lean. So can poor soil conditions. And, of course a fence with improperly set posts will eventually lean of its own weight, no matter what. Bringing a leaning fence back to plumb is not difficult, but it's not a job you want to rush.

The key is digging on the back side of the post sufficiently so it has space in the ground to move (straighten) into. You'll need to dig down to at least ⅔ of the post depth to give it the freedom it needs. If you leave the excavation short, you'll force the bottom of the post to move against solid ground, and that risks snapping it. Concrete footings increase the difficulty of removing the soil, but they don't make it impossible.

There is no hard and fast guide for judging when the excavation is deep enough. On-site field experience is the best guide. You'll know when you begin to straighten the posts. If you get to a point where one or more posts are

almost, but not quite, plumb, loosen the braces, dig a little deeper, pull the fence back again, and rebrace it. With patience, and by working one step at a time, you'll be able to reset the fence exactly as it should be. When you're pulling the posts, you'll hear the fence creak, but if you hear sharp snapping noises, stop and dig some more.

A fence seldom leans in only one bay, so in most cases you'll have more than one post to straighten. Dig around all leaning posts–plus one more, even if the additional one is straight. Pulling the errant posts back into position may leave the next post "overcorrected." Excavating this post will avoid this problem and allow the fasteners a little more "give."

In most cases you'll have to work up and down the leaning section more than once. Trying to straighten the fence in one pass puts too much strain on the wood, and you may end up with a broken rail. Drive metal pipes behind each post as shown in Step 3. That way you can move back and forth along the line without having to reset the pipe.

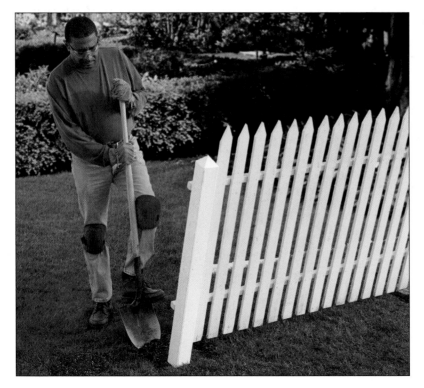

1 To straighten a fence section, start by enlarging the posthole opposite the direction of the "lean" of the fence. Dig down to the base of the post if possible. In most cases a leaning fence will be caused by more than one errant post—enlarge the holes of all posts that are not plumb. If the posts are set in concrete footings, enlarge the holes on all sides of the footings and dig to the bottom.

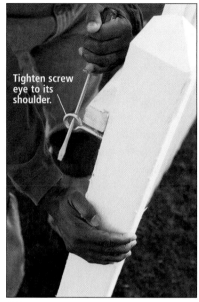

2 Predrill the side or back of each post for a ¼-inch screw eye. Insert the screw eye fully in the post and tighten it by hand as much as possible. Then lever it to its shoulder with a screwdriver inserted through the hole. If the leaning section of the fence is more than two bays long, fasten the screw eye to the innermost post first and start Step 3 at this post.

3 Drive a steel bar or pipe at least 2 feet into the soil, about 4 feet back from the post and angled at 45 degrees. Attach one end of a come-along to the screw eye and the other to the steel pipe. Take up the slack in the come-along and reposition the cable on the pipe as high as possible. Tighten the come-along until the post is plumb and brace the post securely in this position. Remove the come-along and pipe and use the same procedure to plumb the remaining posts.

4 Because straightening the remaining posts may throw the first posts out of line, check each post and replumb them if necessary. Make sure all the holes are wide and deep enough to accommodate a sufficient amount of concrete, enlarging them if necessary. Dampen the surface of any existing footings and backfill the holes with tamped concrete. Let the concrete cure and remove the braces. Retighten or replace any rail or infill fasteners that have worked loose.

Fixing Sagging Gate Posts

Gate posts are the hardest-working members of a fence frame. They have to support the weight of the gate, put up with thousands of openings and closings, absorb the force of the latch hitting the striker plate, and, in some situations, withstand the effects of young people swinging on them. If the hinges hold, all this abuse is transferred to the gate posts.

Gate posts will sag either toward the gate opening or perpendicular to it (or both), and not always just on the hinge side. If the post leans into the opening, you may be able to get by with pulling it back into place with a sag bar– a kit that includes a turnbuckle, a pair of threaded rods, and fasteners. In many cases pulling the post back with a sag bar will also pull it off plumb at right angles to the fence.

To straighten a post leaning perpendicular to the fence, you must give the gate-post base space in which to move. This means digging–down to at least ⅔ of the depth of the post. If the posts are set with concrete collars, break the collars up and remove them with a cold chisel and small sledge. If they're set in concrete footings, don't break up the footings–enlarge the hole by about one-third of its width and excavate to at least ⅔ of its depth. If you find a rotted post base when you dig, you'll have to replace the post (see page 154).

To keep the post from sagging in the future, shore it up with a concrete base. Excavating a trench between the posts and pouring concrete will create a solid base that anchors both posts in all directions.

1 To straighten leaning gate posts, dig around and between the posts so they will have a space to move into when you straighten them. If the posts are set in concrete, dig around the footings.

Use turnbuckle to straighten post leaning into gate opening.

2 Push the post plumb or pull it into position with an iron pipe and come-along (see page 159) and brace it. If the post leans into the gate opening, bring it plumb with a sag bar and turnbuckle. Brace the post in position.

3 Shovel a 4-inch layer of gravel into the excavation to allow water to drain out of it.

4 Tamp the gravel base with a garden rake or tamper and then fill the excavation with concrete. Slope the concrete from the center to all four sides to let water run off. When the concrete cures, remove the braces (but leave the turnbuckle if possible).

MAKING GATE REPAIRS

A sagging gate can be caused by any number of failures in the gate system. Over time the gate may fall out of square, or its hinges can become loose or bent. The longer you let the problem go, the more damage the gate will incur. It is better to fix a minor problem as soon as you discover it than to have to rebuild and replace the gate entirely.

The most common gate problem is loose hinges, or more specifically, loose hinge fasteners. Before repairing the fasteners, however, take a close look at the hinge pins. Grab the gate by the top rail on the latch side and move it slowly up and down. Watch the hinge pins as you move the gate. If they move back and forth or if the fingers of the hinge rock against each other, the hinge is too worn for further use. Then look for bent hinges–a sure sign that the hinges are too small or are not positioned correctly on the gate or post. Gates that are more than 5 feet high or 3 feet wide need to be hung on three hinges–two won't do.

Replace all the hinges, even if only one is worn or bent. One worn hinge means that the other has been working overtime and is soon likely to exhibit the same effects. When you install the new hinges, take a little extra time and mortise them into the posts and gate frame.

Mortising transfers more stress to the entire frame and lightens the load placed on the hinges and fasteners.

When hinge screws have worked loose, it's usually too late to try to tighten them. By this time the screws have probably worn away too much wood, and they won't hold if you do tighten them.

You can move the hinges to a new position on the gate and post (and thus fasten them into fresh wood) but that can disrupt the balance of the gate as well as its aesthetic appeal. Instead remove the hinge pins and the gate and then remove the hinge fasteners from the gate and the post. Drill out the fastener holes as shown below and drive in glued dowels. The dowels provide a strong medium into which to drive the screw. If you replace the screws with longer ones, make sure the head seats properly in the recess of the hinge plate. A protruding screwhead will come into contact with the other hinge plate and stress the gate when you try to open it.

If your gate is large and the hinges too small, you may want to increase the size of the hinges and use machine bolts to support them (see illustration, opposite).

REPAIRING FASTENER HOLES

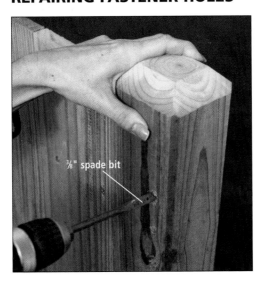

⅜" spade bit

1 To repair fastener holes that have become enlarged by loose screws or nails, remove the gate and old fasteners and drill out the holes with a ⅜-inch spade bit. Because loose holes on the post likely mean loose holes on the gate frame, drill out the holes on the gate too. In both cases drill to a depth about one-half to two-thirds the thickness of the post or gate-frame stock.

2 Cut ⅜-inch dowels about ¼ inch longer than the depth of the holes and coat them with polyurethane glue (it's waterproof and very strong). Drive the dowels into the holes and let the glue dry. With a chisel shave the dowels flush with the surface of the wood.

3 Use a center punch or awl to dent the center of the dowel (the end of the dowel will be harder than the surrounding wood). Predrill it with a twist drill bit the same size as the shank of the new screw. Fasten the hinge with treated screws (nails may split the wood).

COUNTERBORING FOR BOLTS

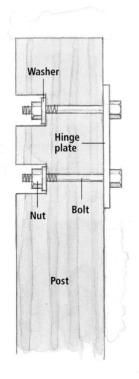

◀ In some cases, especially with a heavy gate, you may want to replace hinge screws with a hefty hinge and bolts. The heads and nuts of machine bolts can sit on top of the face of fence framing, but they will look dressier if you countersink them. Use the techniques shown on pages 118–119 to drill the counterbore and the hole for the bolt. Make sure the counterbored recess is wide enough to accommodate a socket wrench and deep enough to accommodate the thickness of the nut and a washer (plus a lock washer if you use one). Tighten the nut till it's snug, then a half turn more.

A racked (out-of-square) gate will show up with any number of symptoms. It may bind, the latch may work hard or not at all, and the vertical members of the gate frame may appear angled to the rails. All of these problems can be fixed by squaring the gate and reinforcing it so it stays that way.

The first step in reshaping the gate is to set a framing square on an outside corner and apply pressure with a clamp on the opposite diagonal. Tighten the clamp until you can't see any "daylight" between the gate frame and both edges of the framing square. Keep the corners square by tacking a 1× brace on an opposite corner. Then use one of the methods illustrated opposite to brace the frame permanently.

If the gate is square but binds when the weather is wet, shave a little wood off the latch side so it clears the post. Gates should typically have ⅛ to ¼ inch of clearance between the frame and the post to allow for expansion.

If the latch binds in any kind of weather, change the placement of the latch or striker. And if the gate shrinks in dry weather to a point that the latch won't catch, you can relocate the latch or replace it with one that has a longer reach.

SQUARING A GATE

1 Although there are several tools that will help you square a racked gate— a come-along, turnbuckle, or band clamp— a pipe clamp will give you the most control. Check the corners of the gate with a framing square to see which way you need to move the gate, then fasten the clamp.

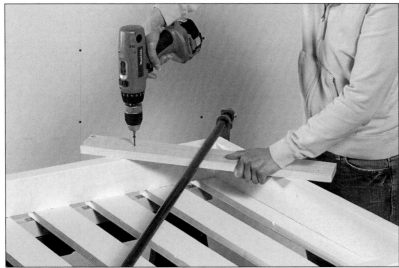

2 Tack a piece of scrap across the corner of the gate to keep it squared. Then remove the pipe clamp and brace the gate with one of several methods shown opposite.

BRACING OPTIONS

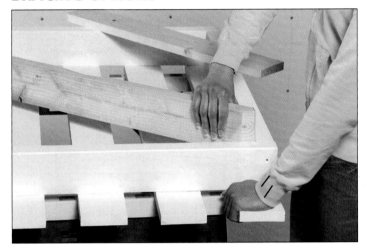

Measure the distance between the corners of the gate and cut a 2×4 with angled ends so it fits snugly in the corners. Fasten the 2×4 brace by driving angled screws into it from the outside of the frame. Remove the temporary brace and rehang the gate.

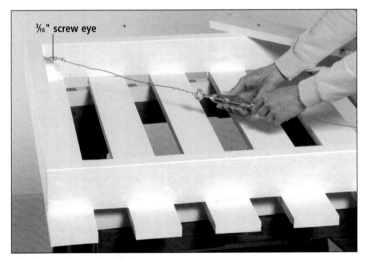

³/₁₆" screw eye

Screw ³/₁₆-inch screw eyes into the corners of the gate and attach a turnbuckle between them. Tighten the turnbuckle till it begins to resist turning. Remove the temporary brace and rehang the gate. After a couple of weeks, check the corners of the gate with a framing square and retighten the turnbuckle if necessary.

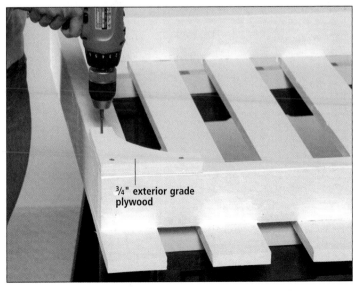

³/₄" exterior grade plywood

Cut decorative corners from ³/₄-inch exterior-grade plywood, then paint them or finish them to match the gate. Fasten them to the corners of the gate with 1³/₄-inch treated screws. Remove the temporary brace, fasten the corner piece, and rehang the gate.

EXTENDING A FENCE LINE

Although extending a fence line in the same plane or perpendicular to an existing fence relies on the same techniques as constructing a new fence, one of the resulting problems is how to get the new surface to match the old.

If your old fence is painted, the problem has an easy solution. Prime and paint the new section to match the old (although you may have to paint both sections to get a perfect match). For stains and other wood finishes, apply a quick-weathering finish or stain that makes the new and old match more closely. Within the period of a year, the two finishes will gradually even out their appearance.

Of the two tasks, extending an addition in the same plane is a little trickier than installing a perpendicular extension. Use the method illustrated, but as an added precaution install batterboards and mason's line perpendicular to the end of the existing fence. Square that line with a 3-4-5 triangle, then use that line to square the extension.

When constructing a perpendicular addition, start it at an existing post or between posts with a mullion as shown.

① To extend a fence line in the same plane as the existing fence, drive a batterboard about 3 feet beyond the end of the proposed extension. Tie mason's line tight between the batterboard and a stake driven about 6 feet before the end of the existing fence. Adjust the line until it's square with an existing post, then measure and mark the new posthole locations. Brace and set the new posts. Use a water level to mark their height, level with the old ones. Cut the posts with a reciprocating saw. Measure down from the top of the posts to mark the rail positions.

② Using the techniques shown on page 132 (for edge rails) or 134 (for flat rails), install the rails on the posts. Then install the infill and finish it to match the existing fence.

INSTALLING A PERPENDICULAR ADDITION

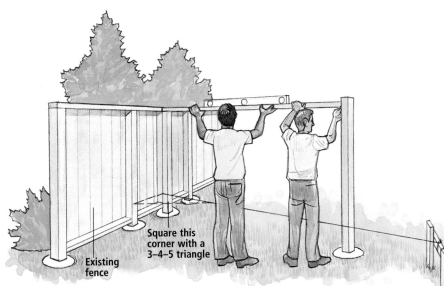

Square this corner with a 3–4–5 triangle

Existing fence

① Attach a 4×4 mullion between the rails and centered on the bay from which you will extend the addition. Tack one end of a mason's line to the mullion and the other to a batterboard set about 3 feet beyond your proposed extension. Square the corner at the mullion with a 3-4-5-triangle. Measure and mark posthole locations, dig the holes, and set the posts. Mark and cut the new posts level with the existing posts.

② Using the techniques shown on page 132 (for edge rails) or 134 (for flat rails), install the rails on the posts. Then install the infill and finish it to match the existing fence.

REPAINTING A FENCE

If you've inherited a fence that needs repainting or if you've come across an old gate you want to set into a new or existing fence, applying a new coat of paint requires some preparation.

The general steps involved in repainting a fence are shown on these pages, but a few additional details may be beneficial.

It's obvious that the best time to repaint a fence is when it begins to crack, chip, or peel. But even if your fence is past that stage, it's easy to save it. What's important is to create a surface that's as smooth and clean as possible—paint will stick better and protect longer.

You can remove the loose paint as shown, feather out the edges with sandpaper, and repaint. These steps will produce an acceptable finish, but you'll always be able to see the places you stripped and those that retain the original coat. Paint hides only a minimal number of blemishes—it accentuates most of them.

If the area you need to repaint is small, you'll get a better-looking and longer-lasting finish if you remove the paint to the bare wood. Here's where a heat gun comes in handy. It softens the paint, making it easier to scrape off. It can burn the wood, so keep it moving.

Even if you remove all the paint, you'll still need to sand the surface smooth. You can use a couple of different sandpaper grits, but you shouldn't need anything finer than a 100 grit.

Because paint won't adhere to oil and grease, wash out greasy spots with a TSP-and-water solution. Be wary of cleaning wood with a power washer. These machines can generate enough pressure that the water spray can remove wood more quickly than a belt sander. Power washing in most cases is overkill and unnecessary. If you do wash the surface with a water-based solution, let the wood dry for several days before painting. A damp surface will bleed through water-based paints and you'll get better adhesion on dry wood. Besides, it's better to brush on a high-quality alkyd paint on outdoor surface. Brushing, by the way, will provide better adhesion than spraying.

1 Scrape off peeling paint with a paint scraper or wide putty knife. If you want to remove all the paint down to the surface of the wood, soften it with a heat gun.

2 Check the surface for any raised or loose nails or screws and reset or replace them.

3 Use a belt sander or random-orbit sander and 80-grit paper to smooth the edges of scraped paint and any rough spots caused by scraping. If you use a belt sander, keep it moving across the surface of the wood to avoid scarring it.

CHECKING FOR LEAD PAINT

Even though production of lead-based paint ceased in 1978, a true mark of its inherent durability is that it's still around on a lot of indoor and outdoor surfaces. And it's a poison. Stripping it mechanically or with a heat process can be hazardous to your health. To check the surface you're refinishing, use an inexpensive swab testing kit. If the test turns positive, use a respirator approved for this purpose by the National Institute for Occupational Safety and Health. Consult your local health department for proper disposal procedures.

4 Prime the wood with a high-quality exterior oil-based primer.

5 When the prime coat is dry, brush on two finish coats of a high-quality exterior alkyd paint.

GLOSSARY

A-D

Actual dimension: The actual physical dimension of a board. See *Nominal dimension*.

Anchor: Metal device set in concrete for attaching posts to footings or piers.

Backfilling: Replacing excavated soil with soil, gravel, or concrete.

Batten: Narrow wood stock tacked to posts to help support level boards.

Batterboard: Layout tool made of two 18-inch stakes and a 24-inch crosspiece.

Bevel cut: An angled cut through the thickness of a piece of wood.

Box nail: Thinner nail than a common nail; drives easier and splits less.

Bubble plan: A plan that includes such nonstructural considerations as view, landscaping features, and traffic patterns.

Building codes: Community ordinances governing materials and construction methods.

Building permit: A license authorizing specified new construction.

Butt joint: The joint formed by two pieces of material fastened at 90 degrees.

Chamfer: To bevel the edges of a piece of lumber.

Check: A crack on the surface or edge of a board.

Clamshell digger: A tool with shovel-like blades and wooden handles used for digging postholes.

Cleat: A length of board attached to strengthen or add support to a structure.

Concrete: A mixture of portland cement, fine aggregate (sand), course aggregate (gravel or crushed stone), and water.

Countersink: To drive the head of a nail or screw so that its top is flush with the surface of the surrounding wood.

Crook: A bend along the length of a board, visible by sighting along one edge.

Crown: A slight edgewise bow in a board.

Cup: A curve across the width of a board.

Dimension lumber: Refers to boards at least 2 inches wide and 2 inches thick.

Dry rot: Fungal growth causing wood to become powdery.

E-K

Elevation drawing: A plan showing the vertical face of a structure, emphasizing footings, posts, rails, and infill.

Finial: An ornament attached to the top of a post or the peak of an arch.

Finish: Any coating applied to wood to protect it against weathering.

Flush: Perfectly level with the adjacent surface.

Frost heave: The upthrust of soil caused when moist soil freezes.

Frost line: The maximum depth to which the ground in your area freezes during winter.

Grade: The surface of the ground.

Heartwood: The center and most durable part of a tree.

Kiln-dried: Lumber dried to a low moisture content to reduce warping.

Kickboard: A board mounted under the bottom rail of a fence and perpendicular to it; used to strengthen the frame and keep animals from crawling under the fence.

L–P

Lag screw: A screw with a hexagonal head that can be driven with a wrench.

Lattice: A material made of crisscrossed pieces of wood or vinyl.

Level: Perfectly horizontal.

Loads: Weights and forces that a structure is designed to withstand.

Mason's line: Twine used to lay out posts, patios, footings, and structures; preferred because it will not stretch and sag as regular string does.

Miter joint: The joint that is formed when two members meet that have been cut at the same angle (usually 45 degrees).

Modular: A term describing a unit of material whose dimensions are proportional to one another.

Mortar: A mixture of one part sand, one part portland cement, and enough water to make a thick paste; used to set stone for patios, walls, and other projects and as grout between stones.

Nominal dimension: The stated size of a piece of lumber, such as a 2×4 or a 1×2.

On-center (OC): The distance from the center of one framing member to the center of the next.

Plumb: Perfectly vertical.

Plumb bob: A tool used to align points vertically.

Prefab: Short for prefabricated, meaning a structure completely assembled and ready for installation.

Pressure-treated wood: Lumber and sheet goods impregnated with chemicals to make the wood moisture-resistant.

R–Z

Rail: A horizontal framing member.

Rebar: Steel rods for reinforcing concrete.

Rip: To saw lumber or sheet goods parallel to the grain pattern.

Rise: The total vertical distance a slope or fence climbs.

Run: The total horizontal distance a fence or slope travels before returning to level.

Sapwood: The lighter-colored, more recent growth of any species of wood used as lumber.

Screening: Maximum opening allowed between railing members; distances vary by code.

Setback: The minimal distance between a property line and any structure.

Shim: A thin strip or wedge of wood used to fill a gap between two materials.

Site plan: A map of your property showing where the fence will be located on your yard.

Small sledge: A sledge hammer, usually 2½ pounds, used where more weight than a carpenter's hammer is needed.

Square: Forming a perfect 90-degree angle.

Stop: 1× or 2× lumber attached to rails to form a frame for inset infill. Also the board that stops the swing of a gate.

Strike: The part of a gate latch fastened to the post.

3–4–5 triangle: An easy, mathematical way to check whether a large angle is square.

Toenail: To drive a screw or nail at an angle.

Water level: Two clear plastic tubes attached to a hose used for establishing level over long distances.

Zoning requirements: Ordinances that regulate the use of property and structure sizes.

RESOURCE GUIDE

AMERICAN LANDMARK FENCE COMPANY

1502 Canton Road

Marietta, GA 30066

770-795-9100

http://www.americanlandmarkfence.com/

CONSOLAID INC.

112 Basaltic Road, Unit 4

Concord, Ontario, Canada L4K1G6

905-669-0861

http://www.flexfence.com/

CALIFORNIA REDWOOD ASSOCIATION

405 Enfrente Drive Suite 200

Novato, CA 94949-7201

888-224-7339

http://www.calredwood.org/

Photographers: Ernest Braun, Tom Rider, Deanna Dikeman, Jim Grove

WYMAN BROTHERS CONST. INC.

105 High Lane

Durango, CO 81303

970-259-9335

http://www.wymanfence.com/

METRIC CONVERSIONS

U.S. Units to Metric Equivalents			Metric Units to U.S. Equivalents		
To Convert From	Multiply By	To Get	To Convert From	Multiply By	To Get
Inches	25.4	Millimeters	Millimeters	0.0394	Inches
Inches	2.54	Centimeters	Centimeters	0.3937	Inches
Feet	30.48	Centimeters	Centimeters	0.0328	Feet
Feet	0.3048	Meters	Meters	3.2808	Feet
Yards	0.9144	Meters	Meters	1.0936	Yards
Square inches	6.4516	Square centimeters	Square centimeters	0.1550	Square inches
Square feet	0.0929	Square meters	Square meters	10.764	Square feet
Square yards	0.8361	Square meters	Square meters	1.1960	Square yards
Acres	0.4047	Hectares	Hectares	2.4711	Acres
Cubic inches	16.387	Cubic centimeters	Cubic centimeters	0.0610	Cubic inches
Cubic feet	0.0283	Cubic meters	Cubic meters	35.315	Cubic feet
Cubic feet	28.316	Liters	Liters	0.0353	Cubic feet
Cubic yards	0.7646	Cubic meters	Cubic meters	1.308	Cubic yards
Cubic yards	764.55	Liters	Liters	0.0013	Cubic yards

To convert from degrees Fahrenheit (F) to degrees Celsius (C), first subtract 32, then multiply by 5/9.

To convert from degrees Celsius to degrees Fahrenheit, multiply by 9/5, then add 32.

INDEX

INDEX

Do-It-Yourself!

Look for these great
home improvement titles
wherever books are sold...

from America's Home and Family authority.

Better Homes and Gardens®

Better Homes and Gardens.
SHEDS & GAZEBOS

Better Homes and Gardens.
decks
Step-by-Step

Better Homes and Gardens.
masonry
& concrete
Step-by-Step

Better Homes and Gardens.
carpentry
& trimwork
Step-by-Step

Better Homes and Gardens.
ADDITIONS